PRACTICE MAKES PERFECT

Basic Hindi

Sonia Taneja

Mc
Graw
Hill

New York   Chicago   San Francisco   Lisbon   London   Madrid   Mexico City
Milan   New Delhi   San Juan   Seoul   Singapore   Sydney   Toronto

मेरे नाना जी एवं नानी जी के लिए

For Gaurav, Katherine, and her generation

1 2 3 4 5 6 7 8 9 10 11 12 13 14 15 16   QDB/QDB   1 9 8 7 6 5 4 3 2

ISBN   978-0-07-178424-5
MHID   0-07-178424-1

e-ISBN   978-0-07-178425-2
e-MHID   0-07-178425-X

Library of Congress Control Number 2011936577

Interior design by Village Bookworks, Inc.
Interior illustrations by Cenveo

McGraw-Hill products are available at special quantity discounts to use as premiums
and sales promotions or for use in corporate training programs. To contact a
representative, please e-mail us at bulksales@mcgraw-hill.com.

Other titles in the *Practice Makes Perfect* series:
Lachance: *Basic English*
Visconti: *Basic Italian*
Richmond: *Basic Spanish*
Kurbegov: *Basic French*
Wochenske: *Basic German*

This book is printed on acid-free paper.

Contents

Preface

Practice Makes Perfect: Basic Hindi is the ideal resource for starting your study of the Hindi language. This book is well suited for anyone interested in beginning to learn Hindi. Whether you are in high school, college, or graduate school or simply want to explore Hindi, this book is the perfect place to start. It can be used either as a primary practice text to accompany a Hindi course or as a supplement to bridge the gap between other Hindi resources.

With eight parts, twenty-five chapters, and more than sixty individual sections, this is a user-friendly workbook that has a variety of features—script practice, accessible grammar, sufficient explanations, practice exercises, categorical vocabulary sets, and cultural information—all in one place. The content is presented in an easy-to-follow sequence that develops from elementary information to complex grammar over the course of eight chapters.

In the first part, a step-by-step approach and specially tailored practice spaces are provided for an easy grasp of the Hindi script. In the second part, user-friendly explanations demystify the complexities of diacritic marks and conjunct characters and enable you to begin reading, writing, and understanding Hindi words. In the next six parts, functional and organized vocabulary sets and tables build a practical vocabulary for day-to-day use. Interwoven with the vocabulary are basic Hindi grammatical tenses and concepts that are explained in an easy-to-understand manner and applied in a variety of exercises.

At various points throughout the text, the Hindi language learning experience is also enhanced by useful cultural notes and insights. Also, for leisure reading, an optional reading and writing practice is given at the end of each part, along with a glossary of new words and relevant cultural information. You can read these at your own pace. Answers to all exercises can be found in the answer key at the back of the book.

Happy Hindi learning!

THE HINDI ALPHABET
पाठ १: हिन्दी वर्णमाला

1. Vowels
2. Consonants
3. Writing consonants
4. Writing more consonants

Grammar

Hindi vowels

Hindi consonants

Vocabulary

Reading practice: Nouns and verbs

Vowels
स्वर

The name of the Hindi script is *Devnagari* (देवनागरी) and, like the English script, it is written from left to right. Unlike the English language, however, Hindi has no capital letters. Moreover, all Hindi letters hang from a straight horizontal line or bar (see below). A letter is not considered complete without this horizontal line attached to it. Hindi is also a phonetic language. None of the Hindi vowels and consonants is silent; each of them is pronounced as it is spelled.

In the Hindi alphabet system, traditionally there are thirteen distinct vowel sounds, although some of them such as ऋ, अं, and अः are omitted in other texts. These are important to know and have been included in this text for complete coverage. Conventionally, there are thirty-eight consonants in Hindi. However, six more sounds occurring in Hindi have been adapted from Sanskrit and Perso-Arabic. As these are useful for new language learners to be able to identify, these have also been shown below.

Hindi vowels at a glance • एक नज़र हिंदी के स्वरों पर

Here are all the vowel sounds that occur in Hindi. They are usually presented in a pattern of alternating short and long sounds.

SHORT		LONG		SHORT		LONG		SHORT		LONG	
अ	a	आ	aa	इ	i	ई	ee	उ	u	ऊ	oo
ऋ	re	ए	ay	ऐ	ai	ओ	o	औ	au		
		अं	un					अः	ah		

Pronunciation • उच्चारण

Following is a pronunciation guide to the Hindi vowels. Phonetic symbols of the IAST (International Alphabet for Sanskrit Transliteration) that are commonly used as a standard for romanizing Indic scripts such as Devnagari have been provided. Sounds and examples in English are there for additional clarification and reinforcement of the accurate pronunciation.

LETTER	PHONETIC SYMBOL	SOUND IN ENGLISH	PRONUNCIATION EXAMPLE IN ENGLISH
अ	a	a	*a* as in *a*mazing
आ	ā	aa	*aa* as in sm*a*rt
इ	i	i	*i* as in *i*s
ई	ī	ee	*ee* as in sp*ee*d
उ	u	u	*u* as in f*u*ll
ऊ	ū	oo	*oo* as in c*oo*l
ऋ	ṛ	re	*re* as in *re*act
ए	e	ay	*ay* as in b*ay*
ऐ	ai	ai	*ai* as in p*ai*d
ओ	o	o	*o* as in *o*cean
औ	au	au	*au* as in *au*spicious
अं	ṃ	un	*un* as in f*un*
अः	ḥ	ah	*ah* as in *ah*oy

Note: Vowels such as ऋ (ṛ) and अः (ḥ) have been adapted from Sanskrit and are more common in words derived from Sanskrit.

EXERCISE

1·1

Match the Hindi vowel with its sound.

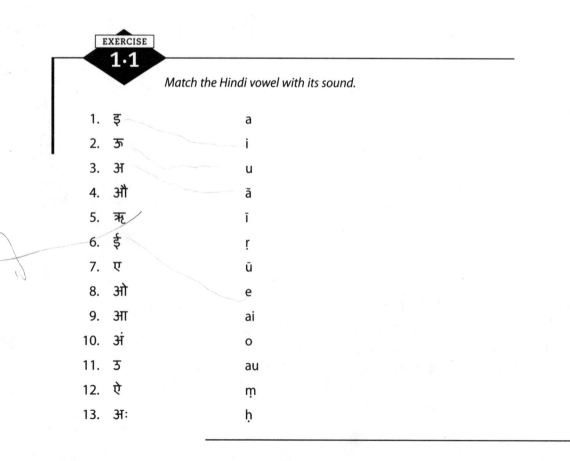

1.	इ		a
2.	ऊ		i
3.	अ		u
4.	औ		ā
5.	ऋ		ī
6.	ई		ṛ
7.	ए		ū
8.	ओ		e
9.	आ		ai
10.	अं		o
11.	उ		au
12.	ऐ		ṃ
13.	अः		ḥ

Script writing practice • लिपि लिखने का अभ्यास

The shape of each letter, and how to write it correctly by hand, is best learned in a step-by-step approach, as presented below. The practice space has been tailored especially for beginner Hindi writers. You can begin by tracing each letter and then proceed to write the letter independently in the space provided. Repeat this process until you develop fluency.

Note that several of the Hindi vowels vary only slightly from each other in their shapes. For example, six out of the thirteen vowels consist of additions made to the first vowel अ (a). It is important to recognize the differences between them. In some cases, variation also exists between the handwritten and print forms. For example, the dots and hooks on the top and side of letters look fairly similar in the handwritten and print versions; however, some marks on top, such as on ऐ, ओ, and औ tend to have an open loop (like a balloon) in the handwritten version. Stark differences in print and handwritten are mentioned where applicable.

At this early stage, the time and practice dedicated to carefully forming the shape of each letter and associating it with its unique sound will pay off in the long run. This knowledge provides a solid foundation for better Hindi reading and writing ability.

Hindi vowels

अ (a)

Progression

3　उ　अ

Practice

अ ─────────

Note that अ sometimes appears as ॲ in print.

आ (ā)

Progression

3　उ　अ　आ

Practice

आ ─────────

इ (i)

Progression

ˈ　ऽ　ॾ　इ

Practice

इ ─────────

ई (ī)

Progression

Practice

उ (u)

Progression

Practice

ऊ (ū)

Progression

Practice

ऋ (ṛ)

Progression

Practice

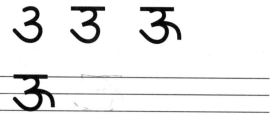

एं (e)

Progression

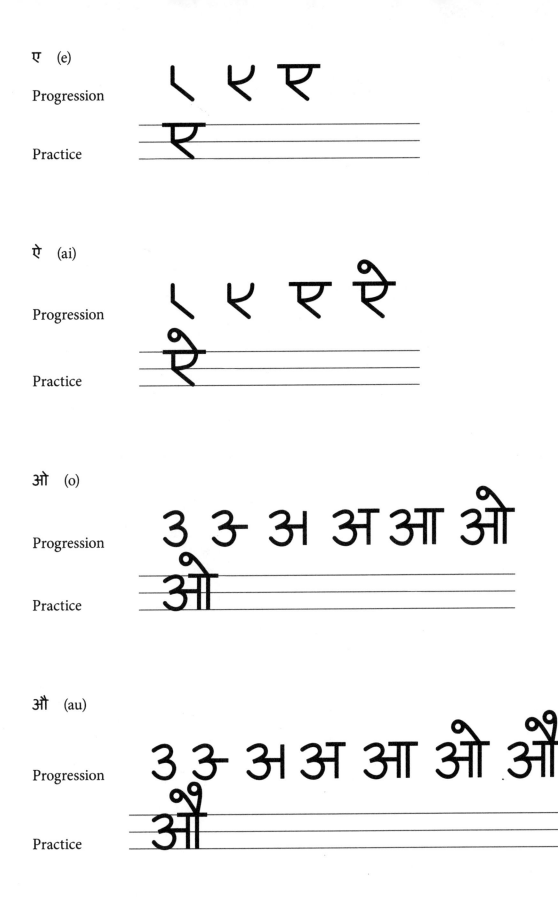

Practice

ऐ (ai)

Progression

Practice

ओ (o)

Progression

Practice

औ (au)

Progression

Practice

अं (ṃ)

Progression

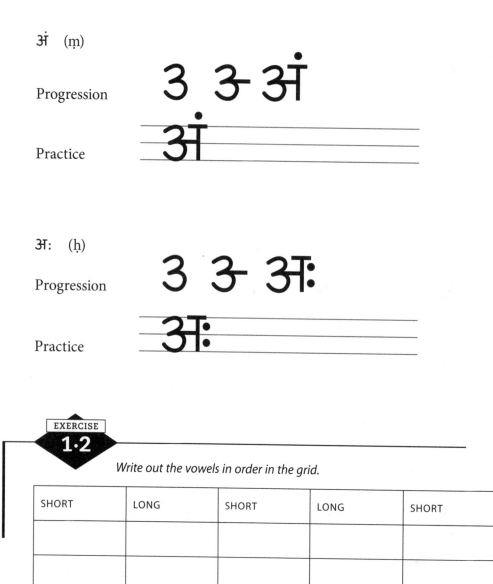

Practice

अं

अः (ḥ)

Progression

Practice

अः

EXERCISE 1·2

Write out the vowels in order in the grid.

SHORT	LONG	SHORT	LONG	SHORT	LONG

Many words in Hindi begin and end with a vowel, although it is rarer to find them in succession of each other. For this reason, before you start reading Hindi, you will have to know the consonants.

Consonants
व्यंजन

The chart below includes the traditional thirty-eight consonant sounds and the six additional consonants that occur in modern Hindi language.

As a memory aide, the consonant sounds are presented in vertical and horizontal groups, according to how they are produced. Vertically, the consonant sounds alternate between unaspirated and aspirated versions and end with a nasal form. For instance, in the first row in the chart below, the first consonant क (ka) is *unaspirated*, which means that it is pronounced without a puff of air accompanying it. The second consonant ख (kha) is *aspirated*, which means that it is pronounced with a puff of air. The third consonant ग (ga) is again unaspirated, followed by the fourth aspirated one घ (gha). This pattern is applicable to the first five rows. Two of the nasals in the chart appear in braces, as they are extremely rare in use.

Hindi consonants at a glance • एक नज़र हिंदी के व्यंजनों पर

	UNASPIRATED	ASPIRATED	UNASPIRATED	ASPIRATED	NASAL	
1	क ka	ख kha	ग ga	घ gha	{ङ} n	Velar
2	च cha	छ chha	ज ja	झ jha	{ञ} n	Palatal
3	ट ta	ठ thha	ड da	ढ dha	ण na	Retroflex
4	त ta	थ tha	द da	ध dha	न na	Dental
5	प pa	फ pha	ब ba	भ bha	म ma	Labial
6	य ya	र ra	ल la	व va/wa		Semi-vowels
7	श sha	ष sha	स sa			Sibilant
8	ह ha					Aspirate/ Glottal

continued

	UNASPIRATED	ASPIRATED	UNASPIRATED	ASPIRATED	NASAL	
A	ड़ rda	ढ़ rda				Dotted version: rolling "r"
B	क़ qa	ख़ kha	ग़ ga	ज़ za	फ़ fa	Dotted version: adapted from Perso-Arabic
C	क्ष ksha	त्र Tra	ज्ञ gya	श्र shra		Combination letters: adapted from Sanskrit

Horizontally, the vowels are grouped according to the part(s) of the human speech organs from which these sounds are generated—the throat, palate, tongue, teeth, and lips.

Velar consonants in the first row are produced at the back of the tongue, in the throat. In the second row, *palatal* consonants are generated using the front of the tongue and the palate. *Retroflex* consonants in the third row are created by folding the tongue to touch the palate and then flipping it forward. *Dental* consonants in the fourth row are produced by the tongue touching the teeth from the inside. In the fifth row, *labial* consonants are generated using the lips. *Semi-vowels* in the sixth row are vowel-like consonants. In the seventh row, *sibilants* are created using a hissing sound that releases air from the mouth. Finally, in the eighth row, the single *aspirate* or *glottal* is produced with a puff of air.

Row A contains retroflex versions of some consonants that have been presented previously in row 3, but occur in a form that is *dotted* at the bottom. The dot adds a rolling "r" to the existing sound. In row B, five dotted versions of the previously presented consonants are shown. These have been adapted from Perso-Arabic and create slightly different sounds. Row C has combination characters that have two sounds within one letter. These have been adapted from Sanskrit.

A more detailed pronunciation guide follows.

Pronunciation • उच्चारण

The IAST phonetic symbols are given below for each consonant. Sounds and pronunciation examples in English are also provided to further distinguish between certain sounds that seem similar when romanized, but are in fact different in Hindi. For example, the vowel ऋ and the consonant ड are both symbolized as "r." In Hindi pronunciation, however, the vowel ऋ is pronounced "re" (as in *react*) and ड is closer to "rda" (as in har*dy*). You may also notice that the sounds in English that have been provided contain an extra "a" at the end of the consonant (ka, kha, ga, etc.). This is because the vowel अ (a) is considered a part of each consonant. This information is important to remember when reading the transliteration and in forming and making a distinction between certain Hindi words later.

LETTER	PHONETIC SYMBOL	SOUND IN ENGLISH	PRONUNCIATION EXAMPLE IN ENGLISH
क	k	ka	*k* as in *k*id
ख	kh	kha	*kh* as in pin*k h*at
ग	g	ga	*g* as in *g*lory
घ	gh	gha	*gh* as in *gh*ost
च	c	cha	*ch* as in *ch*arity
छ	ch	chha	*chh* as in tea*ch h*er
ज	j	ja	*j* as in *j*udge
झ	jh	jha	as in hu*g*e *h*orse

ट	ṭ	ta	*t* as in *t*able
ठ	ṭh	thha	as in po*t h*ole
ड	ḍ	da	*d* as in *d*ouble
ढ	ḍh	dha	*dh* as in re*d h*at
ण	ṇ	na	*n* as in li*n*k, but a heavier sound
त	t	ta	as in si*t th*ere
थ	th	tha	*th* as in mo*th*
द	d	da	*d* as in bandwi*d*th
ध	dh	dha	an aspirated *dha* sound
न	n	na	*n* as in li*n*k
प	p	pa	*p* as in *p*apa
फ	ph	pha	*ph* as in cam*p h*ill
ब	b	ba	*b* as in *b*est
भ	bh	bha	*bh* as in lam*b h*ill
म	m	ma	*m* as in *m*ama
य	y	ya	*ya* as in *y*acht
र	r	ra	*r* as in *r*est
ल	l	la	*l* as in *l*ove
व	v	v/w	*v* as in *v*ision/*w* as in *w*onder
श	ś	sha	*sh* as in *sh*ed
ष	ṣ	sha	same sound as श
स	s	sa	*s* as in *s*and
ह	h	ha	*h* as in *h*ope
ड़	ṛ	rda	*rd* as in ha*rd*y
ढ़	ṛh	rdha	*rdh* as in ha*rd h*at
क़	ḳ	qa	*q* as in s*q*uash
ख़	ḳh	kha	*ch* as in Ba*ch*
ग़	ġ	ga	*g* as in *g*ander
ज़	z	za	*z* as in *z*ap
फ़	f	fa	*f* as in *f*risbee
क्ष	kṣ	ksha	the *ksh* sound in a*cti*on
त्र	tr	tra	the soft trill sound as in the French *tr*ès
ज्ञ	jñ	gya	*gy* sound as in bi*g y*arn
श्र	śra	shra	*shr* as in *shr*ine

Choose the Hindi letter that best represents the English sound.

1. *gh* as in *gh*ost
   a. क   b. ख   c. ग   d. घ

2. *k* as in *k*id
   a. क   b. ख   c. ग   d. घ

3. *jh* sound as in hu*ge h*orse
   a. ज   b. झ   c. ट   d. ठ

4. *g* as in *g*lory
   a. क   b. ख   c. ग   d. घ

5. *ch* sound as in tea*ch h*er
   a. छ   b. प   c. ल   d. र

6. *ḍh* as in re*d h*at
   a. ड   b. ढ   c. ण   d. त

7. *ṭh* as in po*t h*ole
   a. ट   b. ठ   c. ड   d. ढ

8. *d* as in bandwi*d*th
   a. ण   b. त   c. थ   d. द

9. *p* as in *p*apa
   a. ध   b. न   c. प   d. फ

10. *m* as in *m*ama
    a. फ   b. ब   c. भ   d. म

Writing consonants
व्यंजन लेखन

Script writing practice • लिपि लिखने का अभ्यास

As with the vowels, the handwritten progression of each of the consonants is shown below as a guide. The consonant shapes can be traced for practice before writing them independently.

Velar

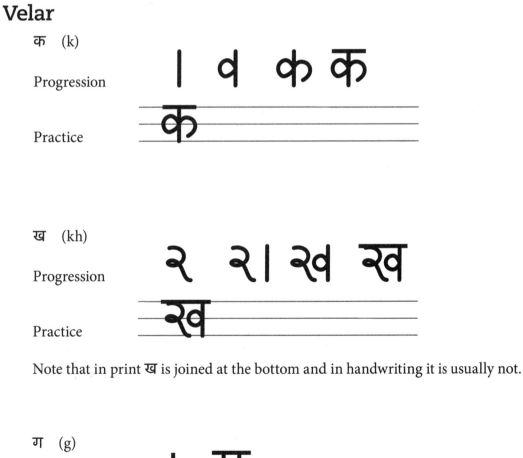

Note that in print ख is joined at the bottom and in handwriting it is usually not.

घ (gh)

Progression

Practice

Palatal

च (c)

Progression

Practice

छ (ch)

Progression

Practice

Note that the end loop touches the horizontal line in print. In handwriting it is usually left at the bottom so that it is not confused with घ.

ज (j)

Progression

Practice

झ (jh)

Progression

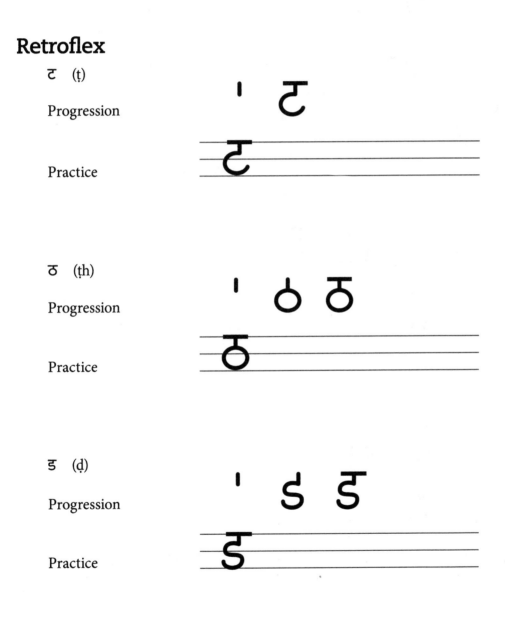

Practice

Note that झ is also written as झ़ in print.

Retroflex

ट (ṭ)

Progression

Practice

ठ (ṭh)

Progression

Practice

ड (ḍ)

Progression

Practice

ढ (ḍh)

Progression

Practice

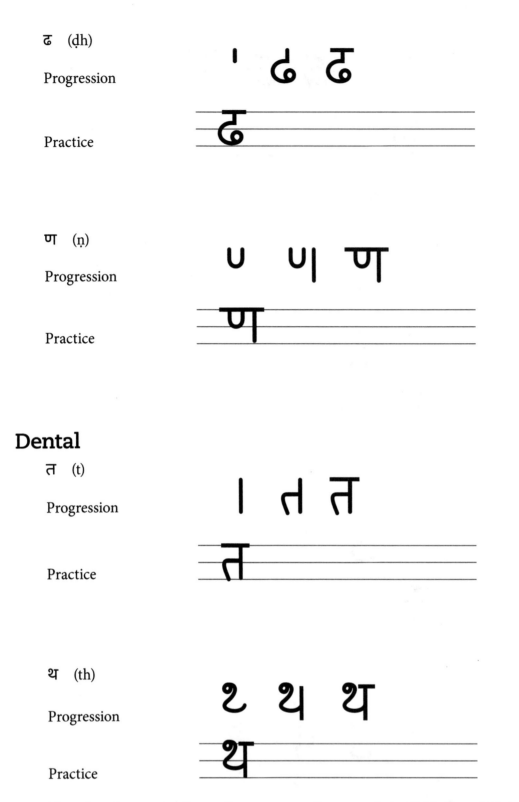

ण (ṇ)

Progression

Practice

Dental

त (t)

Progression

Practice

थ (th)

Progression

Practice

Note that the starting loop of a consonant, for example in थ, ध, भ, and श, is not covered by the horizontal bar.

द (d)

Progression

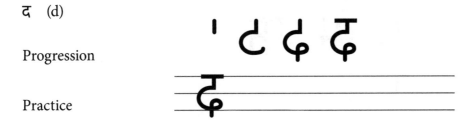

Practice

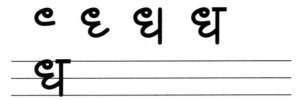

ध (dh)

Progression

Practice

न (n)

Progression

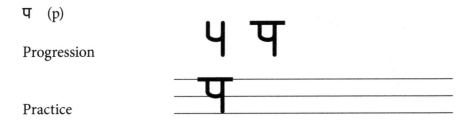

Practice

Labial

प (p)

Progression

Practice

फ (ph)

Progression

Practice

ब (b)

Progression

Practice

भ (ph)

Progression

Practice

म (m)

Progression

Practice

Review the consonants learned so far by matching them with their sound.

1. क   c

2. ख   j

3. ग   g

4. घ   k

5. च   gh

6. छ   jh

7. ज   ṭ

8. झ   ch

9. ट   kh

Review the consonants learned so far by matching them with their sound.

1. ठ   ṭh

2. ड   d

3. ढ   ḍ

4. ण   ḍh

5. त   n

6. थ   dh

7. द   th

8. ध   t

9. न   ṇ

Writing more consonants
अधिक व्यंजन लेखन

Let us continue with the remaining consonants.

Script writing practice • लिपि लिखने का अभ्यास

Semi-vowels

य (y)

Progression

Practice

र (r)

Progression

Practice

ल (l)

Progression

Practice

व (v)

Progression

Practice

Sibilant

श (ś)

Progression

Practice

ष (ṣ)

Progression

Practice

स (s)

Progression

Practice

Aspirate/Glottal

ह   (h)

Progression

Practice

Dotted letters

ड़   (r̩)

Progression

Practice

ढ़   (r̩h)

Progression

Practice

क़   (k̩)

Progression

Practice

ख (k̲h)

Progression

Practice

ग (ġ)

Progression

Practice

ज़ (z)

Progression

Practice

फ़ (f)

Progression

Practice

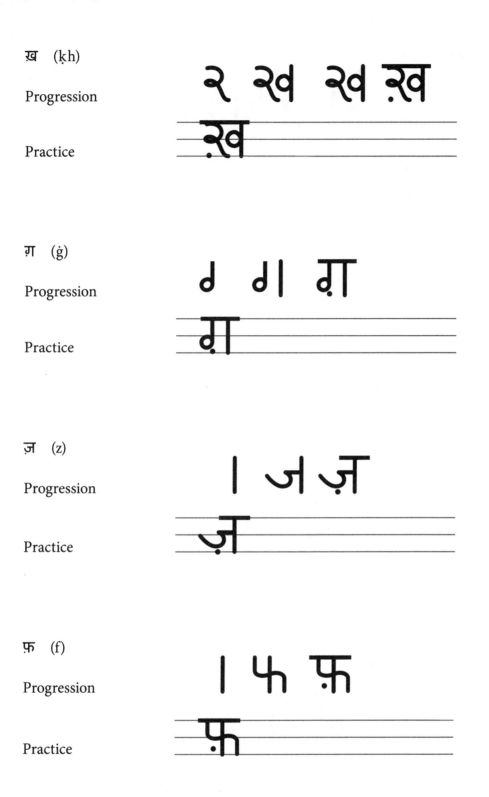

Combination letters

क्ष (kṣ)

Progression

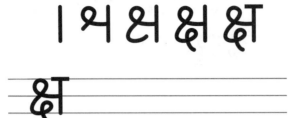

Practice

क्ष

त्र (tr)

Progression

Practice

त्र

ज्ञ (jñ)

Progression

। ज ज्ञ ज्ञ

Practice

ज्ञ

श्र (śra)

Progression

। श श्र श्र

Practice

श्र

Review the second batch of consonants by matching them with their sounds.

1.	ब		r
2.	भ		h
3.	म		v
4.	य		bh
5.	र		ś
6.	ल		ṣ
7.	व		m
8.	श		y
9.	ष		l
10.	ह		ṛ
11.	ड़		b

Review the remaining consonants by matching them with their sounds.

1.	ढ़		kṣ
2.	क्र		śra
3.	ख़		jñ
4.	ग़		k̲h
5.	ज़		k̲
6.	फ़		ġ
7.	क्ष		ṛh
8.	त्र		tr
9.	ज्ञ		z
10.	श्र		f

Now you are ready to test your grasp of all the vowels and consonants together.

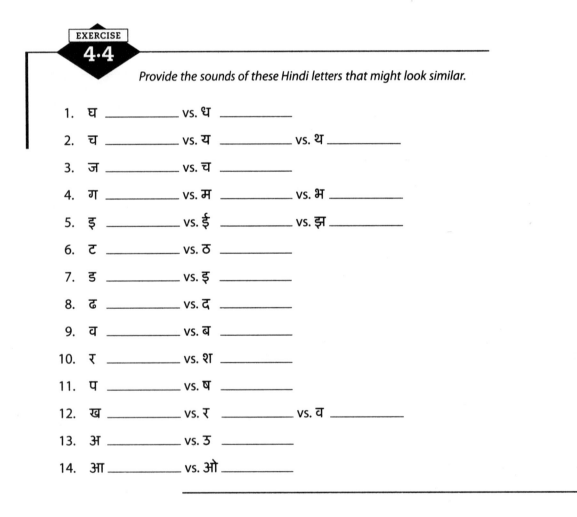

EXERCISE 4·3

Circle the letter that does not belong in the pattern.

1. क फ ख ग घ
2. य च छ ज झ
3. ट ठ र ड ढ ण
4. त थ श द ध न
5. प फ़ स ब भ म
6. य ङ र ल व
7. ञ श ष स ह

EXERCISE 4·4

Provide the sounds of these Hindi letters that might look similar.

1. घ _____ vs. ध _____
2. च _____ vs. य _____ vs. थ _____
3. ज _____ vs. च _____
4. ग _____ vs. म _____ vs. भ _____
5. इ _____ vs. ई _____ vs. झ _____
6. ट _____ vs. ठ _____
7. ड _____ vs. इ _____
8. ढ _____ vs. द _____
9. व _____ vs. ब _____
10. र _____ vs. श _____
11. प _____ vs. ष _____
12. ख _____ vs. र _____ vs. व _____
13. अ _____ vs. उ _____
14. आ _____ vs. ओ _____

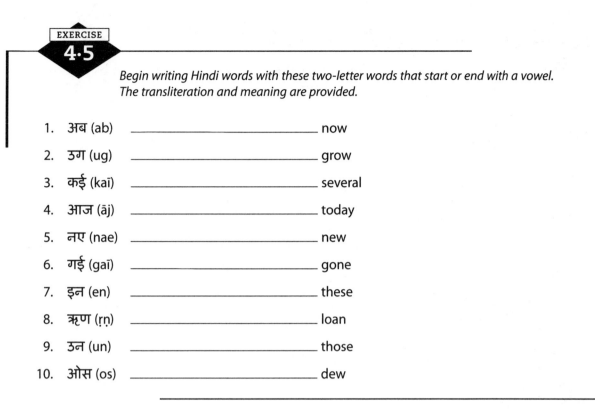

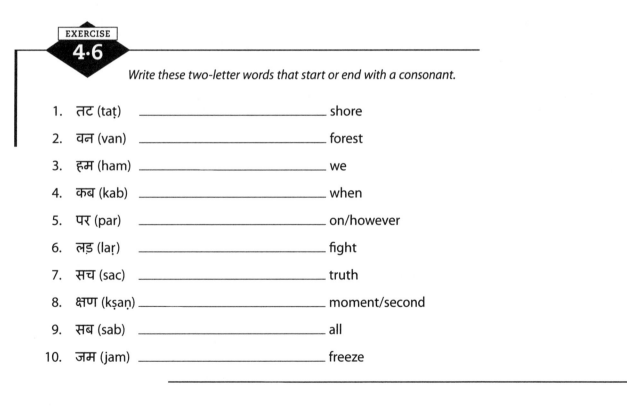

Reading practice • पढ़ने का अभ्यास

For added practice, provide the transliteration of these two-letter nouns and verbs that contain a mix of both the consonants and vowels. This time, only the meanings are given.

Nouns

1. आम _____ mango

2. घर _____ home

3. छत _____ roof or ceiling

4. जल _____ water

5. नल _____ faucet

6. ऊन _____ wool

7. श्रम _____ labor

8. बस _____ bus

9. हक़ _____ right(s)

Verbs

1. पढ़ _____ read

2. कर _____ do

3. चल _____ walk

4. रख _____ keep

5. हट _____ shoo

6. चख _____ taste

7. ढल _____ set (as in the sun)

8. थक _____ become tired

9. फ़ट _____ burst

10. ढक _____ cover

HINDI WORDS
पाठ २: हिन्दी शब्द

Grammar

Diacritic marks
Conjunct characters

Vocabulary

Useful words and phrases
Reading practice: Vocabulary

Culture

Reading Practice: Introductory dialogue

Diacritic marks
स्वर चिन्ह

In Part I, you began to see how Hindi words are formed using vowels and consonants. Another way Hindi words are constructed is by combining a consonant with a particular diacritic mark or symbol (स्वरचिन्ह: svarcinh) associated with a vowel. This means that each of the thirteen vowels shown in Part I has a unique symbol that represents that vowel sound when it is joined with a consonant.

Reading and writing with diacritic marks • मात्राओं के साथ पढ़ना और लिखना

About अ: From Part I, you may remember that the sounds in English (not the phonetic symbols) provided for each of the consonants contained an extra *a*, such as in *ka, kha, ga*. This is because the first vowel अ is already part and parcel of each consonant. This means that the first vowel अ is not added as a diacritic mark because it is already there!

The diacritic mark (मात्रा: mātrā) or accent representing other vowels are shown below. The empty dotted circle indicates the location of the consonant. An important point to note about the pronunciation is that the vowel sound always follows the consonant, even if the diacritic mark appears to the left of the consonant.

NAME (PRONUNCIATION)	SYMBOL
आ की मात्रा (ā kī mātrā):	ा
Placed after the consonant. Example:	का
इ की मात्रा (i kī mātrā):	ि
Placed before the consonant. Example:	कि
ई की मात्रा (ī kī mātrā):	ी
Placed after the consonant. Example:	की
उ की मात्रा (u kī mātrā):	ु
Placed under the consonant. Example:	कु
ऊ की मात्रा (ū kī mātrā):	ू
Placed under the consonant. Example:	कू

continued

NAME (PRONUNCIATION)	SYMBOL
ऋ की मात्रा (ṛ kī mātrā): Placed under the consonant. Example:	ृ कृ
ए की मात्रा (e kī mātrā): Placed above the horizontal line of the consonant. Example:	े के
ऐ की मात्रा (ai kī mātrā): Placed above the horizontal line of the consonant. Example:	ै कै
ओ की मात्रा (o kī mātrā): Placed after the consonant. Example:	ो को
औ की मात्रा (au kī mātrā): Placed after the consonant. Example:	ौ कौ
अं (ṃ, अनुस्वार—anusvār): Placed above the horizontal line of the consonant. Example:	ं कं
There is an additional diacritic mark that is also a nasal sound. अँ (ṃ, चंद्र बिंदु—Candra bindu): Placed above the horizontal line of the consonant. Example:	ँ कँ
अः (ḥ, विसर्ग—Visarg): Placed beside the consonant. Example:	ः कः

Using diacritic marks with consonants • मात्राओं का व्यंजनों के साथ प्रयोग

There is a standard way in which these marks are joined with the consonants. This pattern remains the same for all the consonants. As an example, the diacritic marks are connected with the second consonant ख and the result is shown:

ख + अ = ख (kha) ख + ए = खे (khay)

ख + आ = खा (khā) ख + ऐ = खै (khai)

ख + इ = खि (khi) ख + ओ = खो (kho)

ख + ई = खी (khī) ख + औ = खौ (khau)

ख + उ = खु (khu) ख + अं = खं (khṃ)

ख + ऊ = खू (khū) ख + अँ = खँ (khṃ)

ख + ऋ = खृ (khṛ) ख + अः = खः (khḥ)

Write the next consonant ग with the diacritic marks and the corresponding sounds that are formed.

1. ग + अ   =   _____
2. ग + आ   =   _____
3. ग + इ   =   _____
4. ग + ई   =   _____
5. ग + उ   =   _____
6. ग + ऊ   =   _____
7. ग + ऋ   =   _____
8. ग + ए   =   _____
9. ग + ऐ   =   _____
10. ग + ओ   =   _____
11. ग + औ   =   _____
12. ग + अं   =   _____
13. ग + अँ   =   _____
14. ग + अः   =   _____

Write the following consonant घ with the diacritic marks and sounds.

1. घ + अ   =   _____
2. घ + आ   =   _____
3. घ + इ   =   _____
4. घ + ई   =   _____
5. घ + उ   =   _____
6. घ + ऊ   =   _____
7. घ + ऋ   =   _____
8. घ + ए   =   _____
9. घ + ऐ   =   _____
10. घ + ओ   =   _____

11. घ + औ   = _____

12. घ + अं   = _____

13. घ + अँ   = _____

14. घ + अः   = _____

Write the consonant द with the diacritic marks and sounds.

1. द + अ   = _____

2. द + आ   = _____

3. द + इ   = _____

4. द + ई   = _____

5. द + उ   = _____

6. द + ऊ   = _____

7. द + ऋ   = _____

8. द + ए   = _____

9. द + ऐ   = _____

10. द + ओ   = _____

11. द + औ   = _____

12. द + अं   = _____

13. द + अँ   = _____

14. द + अः   = _____

For complete mastery of this concept, practice the pattern on your own with other consonants.

Exceptions

There are three important exceptions to the standard pattern:

1. With the consonant र, र + उ = रु (ru) and र + ऊ = रू (rū). In this exception, उ and ऊ are not placed below the consonant, but on its side.

2. Similarly, with the consonant ह, ह + ऋ = हृ (hṛ), the diacritic is placed on its side.

3. ऋ is almost never seen combined with other Sanskrit consonants क्ष, त्र, and ज्ञ.

Identify the sounds produced by the following consonants with diacritic marks.

1. ची _____   छै _____   छु _____

2. ठु _____   ड़ू _____   ढी _____

3. थि _____   भि _____   भौ _____

4. लु _____   रु _____   रू _____

5. शी _____   हु _____   ह _____

6. क्षु _____   श्रृ _____   स _____

Now you are ready to start reading, writing, speaking, and understanding a wider array of Hindi words.

Rewrite the following two-letter words according to the vowel and its diacritic mark.

फ़िर, लाभ, शुभ, गृह, वीर, देश, रोज़, सैर, शौक, रंग, धन, नूर, अतः, मुँह

1. अ _____

2. आ _____

3. इ _____

4. ई _____

5. उ _____

6. ऊ _____

7. ऋ _____

8. ए _____

9. ऐ _____

10. ओ _____

11. औ _____

12. अं _____

13. अँ _____

14. अः _____

Following is a vocabulary list of objects you might find in your room.

book	किताब (kitāb)	drinking glass	गिलास (gilās)
shoes	जूते (jute)	clothes	कपड़े (kapaṛe)
one laptop	एक लैपटाप (ek laipṭop)	two tables	दो मेज़ (do mez)
pen	क़लम (k̤alam)	some papers	कुछ काग़ज़ (kuch kāġaz)
key	चाबी (cābī)	water bottle	पानी (*water*) की (*of*) बोतल (*bottle*) (pānī kī botal)

Provide the Hindi word for the following objects.

1. clothes _____

2. two tables _____

3. pen _____

4. some papers _____

5. book _____

6. shoes _____

7. key _____

8. one laptop _____

9. water bottle _____

10. drinking glass _____

Conjunct characters I
संयुक्त अक्षर १

Reading and writing with conjunct characters • संयुक्ताक्षरों के साथ पढ़ना और लिखना

While a diacritic mark is used to combine a vowel with a consonant in Hindi, a *conjunct* character is used to join a consonant with another consonant. Essentially, a conjunct letter is one half of a consonant. In sounding out Hindi words, the presence of a conjunct is often detectable. It usually contains a shorter sound of the consonant being halved, although, to avoid wrong guesses, it is always best to know the spelling of the word.

With conjunct letters, the goal is to know which half of the letter is kept in the script and which half is discarded. It would be too cumbersome for learners to memorize yet another half shape of each letter in the alphabet. So, to make this concept easier to grasp, the conjuncts have been grouped in three basic categories, depending on their basic shape.

Category I consonants are highlighted in the chart below. For a quicker understanding, some of the Hindi and Perso-Arabic consonants with the same basic shape that differ by a dot (for example, क & क़) have been clustered together. The consonants whose conjuncts do not occur very often appear in gray.

क & क़	ख & ख़	ग & ग़	घ	
च	छ	ज & ज़	झ	
ट	ठ	ड	ढ	ण
त	थ	द	ध	न
प	फ & फ़	ब	भ	म
य	र	ल	व	
श	ष	स		
ह				
ड़	ढ़			
क्ष	त्र	ज्ञ	श्र	

Category I: Conjuncts of consonants with a vertical line in the middle

Note: An accent (हलन्त) at the bottom of the consonant (क्) always indicates the conjunct of that consonant. For each consonant, examples show how the conjunct is achieved in the final word.

क and क़

Examples: क् + या = क्या (kyā) *what*   व + क़ + त = वक़्त (vaḳt) *time*

Practice

ख and ख़

Examples: सं + ख् + या = संख्या (saṃkhyā) *number*   ख़् + वा + ब = ख़्वाब (khwāb) *dream*

Practice

ग and ग़ (conjunct rare in ग form)

Examples: ग् + वा + ला = ग्वाला (gvālā) *milkman*   म + ग़ + ज़ = मग़्ज़ (maġz) *brain*

Practice

घ

Examples: वि + घ् + न = विघ्न (vighn) *obstruction*   कृ + त + घ् + न = कृतघ्न (kṛtaghn) *grateful*

Practice

च

Examples: ब + च् + चा = बच्चा (baccā) *child*   अ + नु + च् + छे + द = अनुच्छेद
(anucched) *paragraph*

Practice
_____   _____
_____   _____

ज and ज़

Examples: सु + स + ज् + जि + त = सुसज्जित   ज़् + या + दा = ज़्यादा (zyādā) *more*
(susajjit) *well-decorated*

Note: As these examples indicate, in cases where the diacritic mark for इ (ि) comes after the conjunct, the diacritic mark is elongated to include the conjunct within.

Practice
_____   _____
_____   _____

झ and झ़ (rare in conjunct form)

Example: झ + झ् + झ + र = झझ्झर
(jhajhar) *water jug*

Practice
_____   _____
_____   _____

ण

Examples: पु + ण् + य = पुण्य (punya) *virtuous act*   घ + ण् + टा = घण्टा/घंटा (ghaṇṭā) *hour*

Practice
_____   _____
_____   _____

त

Examples: प + त् + ता = पत्ता (pattā) *leaf*   स + त् + य = सत्य (satya) *truth*

Practice
_____   _____
_____   _____

Note: As the example shows, sometimes when a conjunct त् is added to a whole त, the conjunct is denoted in the word with a line on the following त, instead of half a त.

ध

Examples: ध् + व + ज = ध्वज (dhwaj) *flag*   ध् + या + न = ध्यान (dhyān) *attention*

Practice
_____   _____
_____   _____

न

Examples: न् + या + य = न्याय (nyāy) *justice*   ग + न् + ना = गन्ना (gannā) *sugarcane*

Practice
_____   _____
_____   _____

प

Examples: स + प् + ता + ह = सप्ताह (saptāh) *week*   प् + या + र = प्यार (pyār) *love*

Practice
_____   _____
_____   _____

फ़

Examples: ह + फ़ + ता = हफ़्ता (haftā) *week*　　मु + फ़ + त = मुफ़्त (muft) *free*

Practice

ब

Examples: ब् + या + ज = ब्याज
(byāj) *interest (on money)*

श + ब् + द = शब्द (śabd) *word*

Practice

भ

Examples: स + भ् + य + ता = सभ्यता
(sabhyatā) *civilization*

अ + भ् + या + स = अभ्यास (abhyās) *practice*

Practice

म

Examples: उ + म् + मी + द = उम्मीद (ummīd) *hope*　　च + म् + म + च = चम्मच (cammac) *spoon*

Practice

य (conjunct does not occur often)

Examples: श + य् + या = शय्या
(śayyā) *bed*

भ + य् + या = भय्या
(bhayyā) *brother* (also spelled: भैया)

Practice
_____   _____
_____   _____

ल

Examples: मू + ल् + य = मूल्य
(mūlya) *price*

क + ल् + प + ना = कल्पना
(kalpanā) *imagination*

Practice
_____   _____
_____   _____

व

Examples: दि + व् + य = दिव्य
(divya) *divine*

व् + या + या + म = व्यायाम
(vyāyām) *physical exercise*

Practice
_____   _____
_____   _____

श

Examples: प + श् + चि + म = पश्चिम (paścim) *west*   अ + व + श् + य = अवश्य (avaśay) *necessarily*

Practice
_____   _____
_____   _____

ष

Examples: गो + ष् + ठी = गोष्ठी (goṣṭhī) *symposium*　　कृ + ष् + ण = कृष्ण (Kṛṣan) *Krishna*

Practice _____　_____

स

Examples: व + य + स् + क = वयस्क (vyask) *adult*　　स + स् + ता = सस्ता (sastā) *cheap*

Practice _____　_____

क्ष

Examples: ल + क्ष् + मी = लक्ष्मी (lakṣmi) *laxmi*　　ल + क्ष् + य = लक्ष्य (lakṣay) *goal*

Practice _____　_____

EXERCISE
6·1

Join the following letters and write the resulting word containing a conjunct letter.

1. रा + ज् + य　　= _____ state (government)
2. स् + थ + ल　　= _____ place
3. र + फ़् + ता + र　= _____ speed
4. शु + ल् + क　　= _____ fee
5. अ + न् + य　　= _____ other
6. म + ध् + य　　= _____ middle
7. सू + क्ष् + म　　= _____ small
8. ल + म् + बा　　= _____ long
9. च + श् + मा　　= _____ eyeglass
10. मु + ख् + य　　= _____ main

Conjunct characters II and III

संयुक्त अक्षर २ व ३

Category II: Roundish consonants with no vertical line in the middle

Category II consonants are highlighted in the chart below. The consonants whose conjuncts are rare appear in gray for reference.

Category II consonants

क & क़	ख & ख़	ग & ग़	घ	
च	छ	ज & ज़	झ	
ट	ठ	ड	ढ	ण
त	थ	द	ध	न
प	फ & फ़	ब	भ	म
य	र	ल	व	
श	ष	स		
ह				
ड़	ढ़			
क्ष	त्र	ज्ञ	श्र	

ट: ट्

Examples: छु + ट् + टी = छुट्टी (chuttī) *holiday*

ख + ट् + टा = खट्टा (khaṭṭā) *sour*

Practice _____

44

ठ: ठ् (does not occur often)

Example: पा + ठ् + य = पाठ्य (pāṭhya) *for study*

Practice

ड: ड्

Examples: अ + ड् + डा = अड्डा (aḍḍā) *station*

ल + ड् + डू = लड्डू
(laḍḍū) *a type of Indian candy*

Practice

ढ: ढ् (does not occur often)

Example: ध + ना + ढ् + य = धनाढ्य
(dhanāḍya) *wealthy*

Practice

द: द्

Examples: स + द् + भा + व + ना = सद्भावना
(sadbhāvanā) *goodwill*

श्र + द् + धा = श्रद्धा (śradhā) *devotion*

Practice

हः ह्

Examples: ह् + र + द + य = हृदय
(hṛday) *heart*

ह् + ष् + ट-पु + ष् + ट = हृष्ट-पुष्ट
(hṛṣṭ-puṣṭ) *well nourished*

Practice _____

Category III: Special cases

1. It is rare to see these consonants in a conjunct form: छ, ड, ढ, फ

2. Three of the adapted Sanskrit consonants are already conjuncts of two consonants. Therefore, they do not occur as a conjunct themselves:

   श्र: श् + र

   त्र: त् + र

   ज्ञ: ग् + य

3. The conjunct of the consonant र has several variations:

   a. One is called रेफ़ (ref) and is represented as a flying ˊ above the horizontal line and its pronunciation precedes its appearance on top of the next consonant. For instance, in the words बर्फ़ (barf) *ice* and पर्दा (pardā) *curtain*, the flying र is noted after the fact, but pronounced before. Here are few more examples with the flying र, but now combined with diacritic marks.

      कुर्सी (kursī) *chair*

      मुर्गे (murge) *roosters*

      ख़र्चों (kharcoṅ) *expenditures* (oblique plural form)

      हर्षोल्लास (harṣollās) *joy*

   b. With consonants with a vertical line in the middle, it is denoted as an accent jutting out on the lower left side of the consonant with which it is combined. Examples: क्रम (kram) *order*; ग्रीष्म (grīṣm) *heat*; प्रातः (prātaḥ) *morning*; फ़्रांसीसी (frānsīsī) *French*; भ्रम (bhram) *illusion*, and so on.

   c. The conjunct र is inherent in adapted Sanskrit consonants त्र and श्र, such as in the words मन्त्री (mantrī) *minister* and श्रम (śram) *labor*.

   d. Another occurs as an inverted lower case "v" (पदेन की मात्रा) under consonants that are round at the bottom. Examples include words like राष्ट्रीय (rāṣṭrīya) *national* and cognates such as ड्रेस (ḍres) *dress*.

Join the following letters and write the resulting word containing a conjunct letter.

1. श + ब् + द   _____ word
2. अ + च् + छा   _____ good
3. ध + न् + य + वा + द   _____ thank you
4. अ + र् + थ   _____ meaning
5. क् + या   _____ what
6. हि + न् + दु + स् + ता + न   _____ Hindustan
7. कृ + प् + या   _____ please
8. शु + कि + र् + या   _____ thank you
9. रा + स् + ता   _____ way
10. उ + म + र्   _____ age

Join the following letters and write the resulting word containing a conjunct letter.

1. हि + न् + दी   _____ Hindi
2. दि + ल् + ली   _____ Delhi
3. रा + ज् + य   _____ state
4. प + र् + श् + न   _____ question
5. उ + त् + त + र   _____ answer
6. शु + द् + ध   _____ pure
7. श + क् + ति   _____ power
8. मु + क् + ति   _____ liberation
9. द् + वा + र   _____ door
10. वि + द् + या + ल + य   _____ school

Guess the conjuncts/diacritic marks from the spelling of the words below and write the word in Hindi.

1. Patr   _____   letter

2. Kitāb   _____   book

3. Mej   _____   table

4. Ghantā   _____   hour

5. Din   _____   day

6. Kakṣā   _____   class

7. Subah   _____   morning

8. Samān   _____   luggage, stuff

9. Vaḳt   _____   time

10. Acchā   _____   good, okay

Useful words and phrases • शब्दार्थ: उपयोगी शब्द व पदबंध

Now that you know how to read and write with diacritic marks and conjuncts, it is time to introduce everyday greetings and conventions to help you start a Hindi conversation. The goal of this section is to provide you with some functional basics that can be learned and used right away. Grammatical concepts will be covered in the later chapters.

नमस्ते (Namaste) is the most common way to greet someone in Hindi. It comes from Sanskrit and the meaning translates into "I acknowledge your being." The response is also "namaste."

Two common ways to introduce yourself are:

* मेरा नाम _____ है। (Merā nām _____ hai.) *My name is _____.*

* मैं _____ हूँ। (Maiñ _____ huñ.) *I am _____.*

In formal contexts, people are addressed using

श्री (śrī) or श्री मान (śrīmān)   *Mr.*

कुमारी (kumārī) or सुश्री (suśrī)   *Ms.*

श्रीमति (śrīmati)   *Mrs.*

Alternatively and in general, the suffix जी (jī) is used after a person's first or last name as a way of indicating respect, for example, *Deepak jī* or *Chopra jī*. It is especially relevant if the person is older than you. If you are not sure about the age of the person, it is always considered polite to refer to someone by adding *jī* at the end of their name. Other family members with special forms of addresses such as mom, dad, grandparents, etc. are also referred to by adding *jī*.

Two ways to introduce someone:

- ये <u>दीपक जी</u> हैं। (Ye <u>Deepak jī</u> haiñ)   *This is <u>Deepak jī</u>.*

- आप दीपक जी से मिलिए। (Aāp <u>Deepak jī</u> se milie).   *Meet <u>Deepak jī</u>.*

Punctuation note

The symbol for a period in Hindi is ।, called the Pūrn Virām (पूर्ण विराम). Jī is also added before answering *yes* or *no*, although in a familiar relationship, sometimes it is dropped and only हाँ (hāñ) or नहीं (nahīñ) is used.

जी हाँ (Jī hāñ)	*Yes*
जी नहीं (Jī nahīñ)	*No*

You can ask:

- आपका नाम क्या है? (āpkā nām kyā hai?)   *What is your name?*
  or आपका क्या नाम है? (āpkā kyā nām hai?)

- आप कैसे हैं? (āp kaise haiñ?)   *How are you?*

You can respond by saying:

- मैं ठीक हूँ। (Maiñ ṭhīk huñ)   *I am okay.*

- मैं अच्छा हूँ। (Maiñ acchā huñ)   *I am fine/good/well.*
  (for a male speaker)

- मैं अच्छी हूँ। (Maiñ acchī huñ)   *I am fine/good/well.*
  (for a female speaker)

Grammatical note

Each noun in Hindi has a male or a female gender. The adjectives and verbs are conjugated based on the gender of the relevant noun. Detailed explanations and practice exercises are included in the upcoming chapters to help you master this concept.

You can extend the conversation:

हिन्दी में _____ को क्या कहते हैं?   *What do you call _____ in Hindi?*
(Hindī meñ _____ ko kyā kahte haiñ?)

हिन्दी में _____ का क्या अर्थ हैं?   *What is the meaning of _____ in Hindi?*
(Hindī meñ _____ kā kyā arth hai?)

क्या आप अँग्रेज़ी जानते हैं?   *Do you know English?*
(Kyā āp añgrezī jānte hain?)

माफ़ कीजिए (Māf kījie)   *Excuse me/Pardon me.*

धन्यवाद (Dhanyavād)   *Thank you.*

or शुक्रिया (śukriyā)   *Thank you.*

आप से मिलकर खुशी हुई।   *Nice/pleasure to meet you.*
(āp se milkar khuśī huī)

फ़िर मिलेंगे। (Fir mileṅge)   *See you later.*

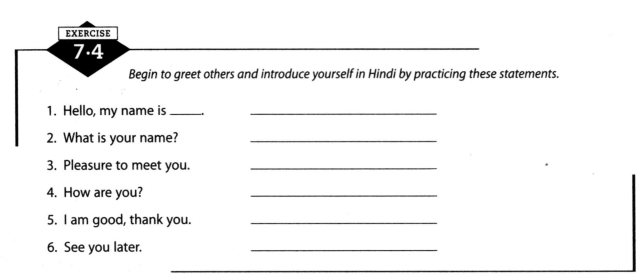

EXERCISE 7·4

Begin to greet others and introduce yourself in Hindi by practicing these statements.

1. Hello, my name is _____.   _____

2. What is your name?   _____

3. Pleasure to meet you.   _____

4. How are you?   _____

5. I am good, thank you.   _____

6. See you later.   _____

Reading practice • पढ़ने का अभ्यास

For added practice, read this short introduction between Dev (a man) and Reena (a woman). New words and phrases are in the following vocabulary list. Translation is in the answer key.

देव: नमस्ते, मेरा नाम देव है। आपका नाम क्या है?
(Dev: Namaste, merā nām Dev hai. āpkā nām kyā hai?)

रीना:   नमस्ते। मैं रीना हूँ। आप कैसे हैं?
(Reena: Namaste, maiñ Reena huñ. āp kaise haiñ?)

देव: मैं ठीक हूँ। और आप?
(Dev: Maiñ ṭhīk huñ. Aur āp?)

रीना:   मैं भी अच्छी हूँ। क्या आप भारत से हैं?
(Reena: Maiñ bhī acchī huñ. Kyā āp bhārat say haiñ?)

देव: जी नहीं, मैं अमरीका से हूँ। आप कहाँ से हैं?
(Dev: Jī nahīñ, maiñ Amrīkā se huñ. āp kahāñ se haiñ?)

रीना:   मैं कैनेडा से हूँ।
(Reena: Maiñ Canedā se huñ.)

देव: अच्छा! आप से मिलकर बहुत खुशी हुई।
(Dev: Acchā! āp se milkar bahut khuśī huī.)

रीना:   मुझे भी। नमस्ते!
(Reena: Mujhe bhī. Namaste.)

देव: नमस्ते।
(Dev: Namaste.)

और आप? (aur āp)	And you?
मैं भी (maiñ bhī)	Me too
मुझे भी (mujhe bhī)	To me too
क्या आप भारत से हैं? (kyā āp bhārat say haiñ)	Are you from India?
मैं अमरीका से हूँ। (maiñ Amrīkā se huñ)	I am from America.
आप कहाँ से हैं? (āp kahāñ se haiñ)	Where are you from?
मैं कैनेडा से हूँ। (maiñ Canedā se huñ)	I am from Canada.

Based on the dialogue, mark these statements either true or false (T/F).

1. Reena is from Stockholm. _____

2. Dev begins the conversation by commenting on the nice weather. _____

3. Reena ends the conversation by saying "see you later." _____

4. Dev is from America. _____

5. At first, Reena asks whether Dev is from India. _____

HINDI SENTENCES
पाठ ३: हिन्दी वाक्य

Grammar

Sentence structure
Subject pronouns
The verb *to be*
The suffix **vala**
Asking and answering *yes/no* questions
Use of *and*, *but*, and *both*

Vocabulary

Nationalities
Vocations
A few common words
Reading practice: Vocabulary

Culture

Cultural notes
Reading practice: Tidbits about famous individuals of Indian descent

Sentence structure
वाक्य रचना

Sentence structure • वाक्य रचना

Compared to English, the sentence structure or syntax in Hindi is quite different. For example, if you wanted to say that Kiran (a female name in Hindi) is Indian, you would say:

किरन भारतीय है। (Kiran bhārtiya hai.)

(Literally) *Kiran Indian is.*

Kiran is Indian.

In a Hindi sentence, the verb is placed toward the end of the sentence. The verb in this case is *to be* (होना—honā) and *is* is है (hai) that agrees with the subject Kiran.

As another example, if you wanted to say that Appu (a character in *The Simpsons*) is American, you would say:

अप्पु अमरीकी है। (Appu amrīkī hai.)

(Literally) *Appu American is.*

Appu is American.

The appropriate conjugation for the verb *to be* (होना—honā), *is* है (hai), is placed at the very end and this conjugation agrees with the subject *Appu*.

Nationalities • शब्दार्थ: राष्ट्रीयताएँ

Afghan	अफ़्गानी (Afgānī)
African	अफ़्रीकी (Afrīkī)
American	अमरीकी (Amrīkī)
Asian	एशियाई (Aśiyaī)
Australian	ओस्ट्रेलियन (Ausṭreliyan)
Bangladeshi	बंगला (Baṅglā), बंगलादेशी (Baṅglādeśī)
Bhutanese	भूटानी (Bhūtānī)
British/English	ब्रितानी (Britānī)/अँग्रेज़ (Aṅgrez)
Chinese	चीनी (Cīnī)
French	फ्रांसीसी (Frānsīsī)

German	जर्मन (Jarman)
Greek	यूनानी (ūnānī)
Indian	भारतीय (Bhārtīya, from भारत, India's name in Hindi) or हिन्दुस्तानी (Hindustānī, from हिन्दुस्तान, another common name for India)
Iranian	ईरानी (Irānī)
Iraqi	ईराकी (Irākī)
Israeli	इज़राईली (Isrāīlī)
Italian	इतालवी (Itālavī)
Japanese	जापानी (Jāpānī)
Nepalese	नेपाली (Nepālī)
Pakistani	पाकिस्तानी (Pākistānī)
Russian	रूसी (Rūsī)
Vietnamese	वियतनामी (Vietnāmī)

EXERCISE
8·1

Match the English with the Hindi equivalents.

1.	German	भूटानी
2.	Vietnamese	ओस्ट्रेलियन
3.	English	जर्मन
4.	Greek	ईराकी
5.	French	ईरानी
6.	Indian	वियतनामी
7.	Bhutanese	यूनानी
8.	Australian	हिन्दुस्तानी/भारतीय
9.	Iraqi	अँग्रेज़/ब्रितानी
10.	Iranian	फ़्रांसीसी

Complete these sentences in Hindi. The first names are already provided.

1. Suki is Japanese.   सूकी   _____

2. David is Israeli.   डेविड   _____

3. Sonia is American.   सोनिया   _____

4. Pema is Nepalese.   पेमा   _____

5. Chao is Chinese.   चाओ   _____

6. Olivier is French.   ओलिविय   _____

7. Hamid is Afghan.   हमीद   _____

8. Nilofar is Pakistani.   नीलोफ़र   _____

9. Shahnaz is Bangladeshi.   शहनाज   _____

10. Michael is British.   माईकल   _____

11. Mario is Italian.   मारियो   _____

12. Vladimir is Russian.   व्लैडिमिर   _____

13. Sophie is African.   सोफ़ी   _____

14. Kiran is Asian.   किरन   _____

Subject pronouns • सर्वनाम

Now that you have learned how to construct a Hindi sentence using a proper noun (the name of a person), it is time to add the personal pronouns:

I   मैं (maiñ)

we   हम (ham)

you   तू (Tū)/तुम (tum)

Cultural notes

◆ तू (tū) and तुम (tum) forms are informal. They are used with relatives and friends similar or younger in age to you, although तू is also used with children and servants and may indicate a lack of respect.

      आप (āp)   *you*

◆ आप (āp) is the formal "you" form used for reverence for elders and others. It is also the generic "you" form used in all public situations. It is considered polite and indicates respect. In the hierarchy of forms for "you" in Hindi, आप (āp) is formal and polite, तुम (tum) is semi-formal and semi-polite, and तू (tū) is the most informal and can indicate a lack of politeness. To avoid confusion, in this text, the formal "you" means आप (āp) and the other forms are treated as informal.

यह (yah)	*this, he, she, it*
वह (vah)	*that, he, she, it*
ये (ye)	*they, these*
वे (ve)	*they, those*

Often, यह/ये (yah/ye) is used with objects and people located near the speaker (hereby referred to as proximity), while वह/वे (vah/ve) is used with objects and people located literally or figuratively away from the speaker (hereby referred to as distance). Colloquially, वह and वे are sometimes used together as वो. वो is both singular and plural.

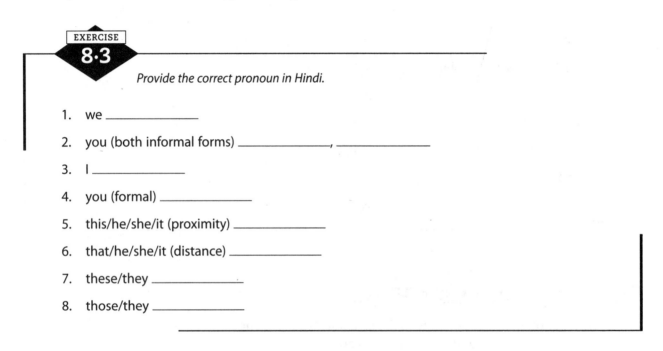

EXERCISE
8·3

Provide the correct pronoun in Hindi.

1. we _____

2. you (both informal forms) _____, _____

3. I _____

4. you (formal) _____

5. this/he/she/it (proximity) _____

6. that/he/she/it (distance) _____

7. these/they _____

8. those/they _____

The verb *to be* • "होना" क्रिया

The verb होना is an important common verb in Hindi. Here is how होना (honā) is conjugated with personal pronouns.

मैं हूँ (maiñ huñ)	*I am*
हम हैं (ham haiñ)	*we are*

Notice the nasal dot in हैं that is the plural of है.

तू है (tū hai)	
तुम हो (tum ho)	*you are*
आप हैं (āp haiñ)	

Cultural notes

For the purpose of conjugation, the formal *you* (आप) is treated as a plural, even when referring to a single person. This concept in Hindi is called the "honorary" plural (आदर वाचक). It also applies to all subjects addressed with Jī (जी).

यह/वह है (yah/vah hai)		*this/that/he/she/it is*
ये/वे हैं (ye/ve haiñ)		*these/those/they are*

Notice again the appearance of the nasal dot to form the plural.

EXERCISE

8·4

Circle the correct conjugation of the verb to be *with the given pronoun.*

1. मैं   हूँ,   हो,   है,   हैं
2. तू   हूँ,   हो,   है,   हैं
3. तुम   हूँ,   हो,   है,   हैं
4. आप   हूँ,   हो,   है,   हैं
5. यह/वह   हूँ,   हो,   है,   हैं
6. ये/वे   हूँ,   हो,   है,   हैं
7. हम   हूँ,   हो,   है,   हैं

EXERCISE

8·5

Conjugate the Hindi verb to be.

1. I am   _____
2. She is   _____
3. He is   _____
4. They are   _____
5. Those are   _____
6. We are   _____
7. You (*informal*) are   _____
8. You (*formal*) are   _____

Vocations • शब्दार्थ: पेशे

accountant	मुनीम (munīm)
actor, actress	अभिनेता (abhinetā, *m.*), अभिनेत्री (abhinetrī, *f.*)
ambassador	राजदूत (rājdūt)
artisan	कारीगर (kārīgar)
artist	कलाकार (kalākār)
bank teller	खज़ांची (khazāñcī)
businessman	व्यवसायी (vyavasāyī)
carpenter	बढ़ई (baṛhaī)
confectioner	हलवाई (halwāī)
dancer	नर्तक (nartak, *m.*), नर्तकी (nartaki, *f.*)
diplomat	राजनायक (rājnāyak)
doctor	चिकित्सक (cikitsak), डाक्टर (ḍakṭar)
driver	चालक (cālak), ड्राइवर (draīvar)
engineer	अभियंता (abhiyantā), इंजीनियर (injīniar)
farmer	किसान (kisān), कृषक (kṛśak)
gardener	माली (mālī)
hairdresser	नाई (nāī)
jeweler	जौहरी (jauharī)
judge	न्यायधीश (nyāydhīś)
laborer	मज़दूर (mazdūr)
lawyer	वक़ील (vakīl)
mailman	डाकिया (ḍākiyā)
mechanic	मिस्त्री (mistrī)
merchant	व्यापारी (vyāpārī)
musician	संगीतकार (saṅgītkār)
nurse	नर्स (nars)
player (football, etc.)	खिलाड़ी (khilāṛī)
police officer	पुलिस अधिकारी (pulis adhikārī)
potter	कुम्हार (kumhār)
president	राष्ट्रपति (rāṣṭrapatī)
prime minister	प्रधानमंत्री (pradhānmantrī)
publisher	प्रकाशक (prakāśak)
salesman	विक्रेता (vikretā)
sculptor	मूर्तिकार (mūrtīkār)
security officer/person	सुरक्षा कर्मचारी (surakṣā karamcārī)
shopkeeper	दुकानदार (dukāndār)

singer	गायक (gāyak, *m.*), गायिका (gāyikā, *f.*)
student	विद्यार्थी (vidyārthī)
tailor	दर्ज़ी (darzī)
teacher	अध्यापक (adhyāpak, *m.*), अध्यापिका (adhyāpikā, *f.*)
thief	चोर (cor)
tourist	पर्यटक (paryaṭak)
washerman	धोबी (dhobī)
writer	लेखक (lekhak, *m.*), लेखिका (lekhikā, *f.*)

Match the English with the Hindi equivalent.

1. thief   नाई 7
2. jeweler   बढ़ई 10
3. sculptor   हलवाई 8
4. mechanic   नर्तक, नर्तकी 9
5. tourist   जौहरी 2
6. musician   मिस्त्री 4
7. hairdresser   संगीतकार 6
8. confectioner   मूर्तिकार 3
9. dancer   चोर 1
10. carpenter   पर्यटक 5

Write the following sentences in Hindi.

1. I am a diplomat.   _____
2. She is a teacher.   _____
3. He is a farmer.   _____
4. They are lawyers.   _____
5. Those are doctors.   _____
6. We are drivers.   _____
7. You (informal) are a mailman. _____
8. You (formal) are a tailor.   _____

Questions and answers
प्रश्न व उत्तर

The suffix **vala** • वाला प्रत्यय

Similar to the English suffix -*er* (for example, toy mak*er*) one of the many uses of the suffix -वाला is to be added to a noun to indicate a relation with that noun such as selling, making, or owning.

Here are a few nouns:

दूध (dūdh, *m.*)	*milk*
सब्ज़ी (subzī, *f.*)	*vegetable*
कपड़े (kapaṛe, *m. pl.*)	*clothes*
फूल (fūl, *m. s./m. pl.*)	*flower*
दुकान (dukān, *f.*)	*shop*
घर (ghar, *m.*)	*home/house*

Adding the suffix वाला creates the relation:

दूधवाला	*milkman*
सब्ज़ीवाला	*vegetable vendor*
कपड़ेवाला	*clothier*
फूलवाला	*florist*
दुकानवाला	*shopkeeper*
घरवाला	*man of the house*

Add the suffix वाला *to the following nouns.*

police	पुलिस (*f.*)	1.	_____	policeman
money	पैसे (*m. pl.*)	2.	_____	rich man
bus	बस (*f.*)	3.	_____	bus driver
toys	खिलौने (*m. pl.*)	4.	_____	toy seller
taxi	टैक्सी (*f.*)	5.	_____	taxi driver

A few common words • शब्दार्थः कुछ आम शब्द

आदमी (ādmī, *m.*)	man, human
औरत (aurat, *f.*)	woman
लड़का (laṛkā, *m.*)	boy
लड़की (laṛkī, *f.*)	girl
दोस्त (dost, *m.*), मित्र (mitr, *m.*)	friend
सहेली (sahelī, *f.*)	gal pal (female friend to a female)
यार (yār, *m.*)	buddy (male friend to a male)
लोग (log, *m. pl.*)	people
चीज़ (cīz, *f.*)	thing
या (yā)	or
वग़ैरह (vagairah)	etc.

Asking and answering yes/no questions • हाँ/नहीं के प्रश्नोत्तर

Questions that begin with *Is* or *Are* in English begin with the interrogative word क्या (kyā) in Hindi. As you learned in the previous chapter, जी हाँ (jī haṅ) means *yes* and जी नहीं (jī nahiṅ) means *no*, although, in familiar contexts, people simply say हाँ (haṅ) or नहीं (nahiṅ).

Look at how questions and affirmative answers are constructed. Is/Are questions begin with क्या (kyā), followed by the statement that is in question and end with the verb *to be*. The affirmative answer begins with जी हाँ (jī haṅ) and essentially restates the statement.

क्या वह आदमी रूसी है? (kyā vah ādmī rūsī hai?)	*Is that man Russian?*
जी हाँ, वह रूसी है। (jī haṅ, vah rūsī hai)	*Yes, he is Russian.*
क्या वे लोग दुकानदार हैं? (kyā ve log dukāndār haiṅ?)	*Are those people shopkeepers?*
जी हाँ, वे दुकानदार हैं। (jī haṅ, ve dukāndār haiṅ)	*Yes, they are shopkeepers.*

Here is how negative answers are formed. The main differences are that the negative answer begins with जी नहीं (jī nahiñ) and the the verb *to be* is negated.

क्या वह औरत फ़्रांसीसी है? (kyā vah aurat frānsīsī hai?)   *Is that woman French?*

जी नहीं, वह फ़्रांसीसी नहीं है। (jī nahiñ, vah frānsīsī nahiñ hai)   *No, she is not French.*

क्या यह लड़का किसान है? (kyā yah laṛkā kisān hai?)   *Is this boy a farmer?*

जी नहीं, यह किसान नहीं है। (jī nahiñ, yah kisān nahiñ hai)   *No, he is not a farmer.*

Transitioning from negations to affirmative answers

For a more complete response, after answering in the negative, the person questioned might provide an alternative, correct answer by starting with जी नहीं (jī nahiñ), negating the statement, providing the different information, and then ending with the verb *to be*.

क्या वह लड़की मुनीम है?
(kyā vah laṛkī munīm hai?)   *Is that girl an accountant?*

जी नहीं, वह मुनीम नहीं, ख़ज़ांची है।
(jī nahiñ, vah munīm nahiñ, khazāñcī hai)   *No, she is not an accountant, (she is) a bank teller.*

क्या वह चीज़ चीनी है? (kyā vah cīz cīnī hai?)   *Is that thing Chinese?*

जी नहीं, वह चीनी नहीं, अमरीकन है।
(jī nahiñ, vah cīnī nahiñ, amrīkan hai)   *No, it is not Chinese, (it is) American.*

EXERCISE
9·2

Translate the following into Hindi to practice asking and answering yes/no *questions.*

1. Are you (*formal*) an artist?   _____

2. Yes, I am an artist.   _____

3. Is that man Indian?   _____

4. Yes, he is Indian.   _____

5. Is that woman an engineer?   _____

6. No, she is not an engineer.   _____

7. Are those people merchants?   _____

8. No, those are not merchants, (those) are diplomats.   _____

9. Are these things Bangladeshi?   _____

10. No, these are not Bangladeshi, (these) are Pakistani.   _____

Use of *and, but,* and *both* • और, पर, और दोनों का प्रयोग

Similar to English, Hindi sentences can be developed by adding some basic connectors such as *and, but,* and *both.*

There are many words for *and* in Hindi: और (aur) is the most common way of saying *and* in conversation. Other words for *and* such as व (v), एवं (evaṃ), and अथवा (athvā) are good to know because these appear in authentic texts such as newspapers, magazines, and other Hindi literature.

विजय और नीरज डाक्टर हैं। (Vijay aur Neeraj dokṭar haiñ)	*Vijay and Neeraj are doctors.*
सीमा और रेचल अमरीकी हैं। (Seema aur Rachel amrīkī haiñ)	*Seema and Rachel are Americans.*

Similarly, there are several words for *but*: पर (par), लेकिन (lekin), and मगर (magar) occur frequently in spoken Hindi, while परन्तु (parantu) and किन्तु (kintu) are used more often in written Hindi.

वह राजनायक है, पर राजदूत नहीं। (vah rājnāyak hai, par rājdūt nahiñ)	*He is a diplomat, but not an ambassador.*
हम चिकित्सक हैं, लेकिन व्यवसायी नहीं। (ham cikitsak haiñ, lekin vyavasāyī nahiñ)	*We are doctors, but not businessmen.*

The word for *both* in Hindi is दोनों and, understandably, it occurs only in plural form.

क्या तुम दोनों मज़दूर हो? (kyā tum dono mazdūr ho?)	*Are you both laborers?*
जी हाँ, हम दोनों मज़दूर हैं। (Jī hañ, ham dono mazdūr haiñ)	*Yes, we are both laborers.*
क्या लिओ और थिओ दोनों यूनानी हैं? (kyā Leo aur Theo dono ūnānī haiñ?)	*Are Leo and Theo both Greek?*
नहीं, लिओ इतालवी है और थिओ यूनानी है। (nahiñ, Leo itālavī hai aur Theo ūnānī hai)	*No, Leo is Italian and Theo is Greek.*

EXERCISE
9·3

Fill in the blanks with and, both, *or* but.

1. ऐन्डरसन कूपर _____ संजय गुसा दोनों अमरीकी हैं।

2. दीपक चोपड़ा चिकित्सक है, _____ वकील नहीं।

3. झुम्पा लहरी और चित्रा बैनर्जी दिवाकरूनी _____ लेखिकाएँ (*writers*) हैं।

4. क्या हम _____ भारतीय हैं?

5. क्या राजीव _____ रेखा कलाकार हैं?

6. जी नहीं, रेखा कलाकार है, _____ राजीव अध्यापक है।

Reading practice • पढ़ने का अभ्यास

For added practice, read tidbits about famous individuals of Indian descent. Useful vocabulary is provided below, and, for further help, the transliteration and meaning can be found in the answer key.

1. अमिताभ बच्चन (Amitabh Bacchan) भारत का एक प्रसिद्ध अभिनेता है।
2. "महात्मा" गाँधी (Mahatma Gandhi) का नाम मोहनदास करमचंद गाँधी था।
3. सबीर भाटिया (Sabeer Bhatia) हॉटमेल का संस्थापक है।
4. मधुर जाफ़री (Madhur Jaffrey) की कई किताबें हैं।
5. मदर टरीसा (Mother Teresa) कलकत्ता में काम करती थीं।
6. गायिका नोरह जोंज़ (Norah Jones) आधी भारतीय है।
7. बॉबी जिंदल (Bobby Jindal) लूईज़ियाना, अमरीका का पहला भारतीय-अमरीकी राज्यपाल है।
8. सुनीता विलियम्ज़ (Sunita Williams) अंतरिक्ष में सबसे लम्बी यात्रा करनेवाली पहली औरत है।
9. मीरा नेयर (Mira Nair) और एम. नाईट श्यामालान (M. Night Shyamalan) दोनों दिलचस्प फ़िल्में बनाते हैं।
10. लता मंगेशकर (Lata Mangeshkar) भारत की एक प्रसिद्ध गायिका हैं।

भारत का/की	India's	राज्यपाल	governor
था/थी	was	अंतरिक्ष में	in space
संस्थापक	founder	सबसे लम्बी यात्रा	the longest journey
कई किताबें	several books	करनेवाली	the one doing
प्रसिद्ध	famous	दिलचस्प	interesting
आधी	half	फ़िल्में बनाते	make films
पहला, पहली	first		

Mark these statements true or false (T/F) based on the information given above.

1. मीरा नेयर और एम. नाईट श्यामालान भारतीय-अमरीकी राज्यपाल हैं। _____
2. अमिताभ बच्चन अंतरिक्ष में सबसे लम्बी यात्रा करनेवाली पहली औरत है। _____
3. नोरह जोंज़ व लता मंगेशकर प्रसिद्ध गायिकाएँ हैं। _____
4. सुनीता विलियम्ज़ कलकत्ता में काम करती थीं। _____
5. मधुर जाफ़री की कई किताबें हैं। _____

THE PRESENT TENSE
पाठ ४: वर्तमान काल

Grammar

The infinitive
The present indefinite tense
Saying dates and age
Possessives

Vocabulary

Some useful verbs
More verbs
Daily routine
Numbers 1–100
Reading practice: Vocabulary

Culture

Cultural notes

The present indefinite
सामान्य वर्तमान

The infinitive verb • क्रियार्थक संग्या

Verbs occur in what is called an infinitive form: *to be, to come, to go*, etc. The infinitive form of Hindi verbs contains a verb stem and ends with the suffix -ना. For example, in the verb जाना (jānā) *to go*, the verb stem is जा (jā) and the suffix is ना (nā).

Some useful verbs • कुछ उपयोगी क्रियाएँ

Here are some useful verbs in the infinitive form, with their verb stem.

to come	आना (ānā, verb stem: आ)
to go	जाना (jānā, verb stem: जा)
to awake	जागना (jāgnā, verb stem: जाग)
to sleep	सोना (sonā, verb stem: सो)
to eat	खाना (khānā, verb stem: खा)
to drink	पीना (pīnā, verb stem: पी)
to bathe, to shower	नहाना (nahānā, verb stem: नहा)
to read, to study	पढ़ना (paṛhnā, verb stem: पढ़)
to write	लिखना (likhnā, verb stem: लिख)
to do	करना (karnā, verb stem: कर)
to see, to watch	देखना (dekhnā, verb stem: देख)
to drive (something)	चलाना (calānā, verb stem: चला)

Match the Hindi verb with its English meaning.

1.	आना	to drink
2.	जाना	to bathe, shower
3.	जागना	to sleep
4.	खाना	to go
5.	पीना	to read, study
6.	सोना	to eat
7.	नहाना	to drive (something)
8.	पढ़ना	to awake
9.	लिखना	to write
10.	करना	to see, watch
11.	देखना	to come
12.	चलाना	to do

Present indefinite tense • सामान्य वर्तमान काल

Review the pronouns and the verb *to be* from the previous chapter.

मैं हूँ

तू है

तुम हो

आप हैं

हम हैं

यह/वह है

ये/वे हैं

As you have already seen in the previous sections, Hindi sentences end with the appropriate conjugation of the basic verb *to be*, depending on the subject. Even as we add other verbs, sentences will still end with the conjugation of the verb *to be*. So, if you wanted to say *she writes* in Hindi, you will use both the conjugation for the verb *to write* and for the verb *to be* with the subject *she*. See detailed example shown below with the verb *to go*.

For the present indefinite tense (example: I go, she sleeps), additional aspects are added—that of gender and number. As you might remember from the different forms of male and female statements provided in the prior chapters, Hindi is a gendered language. In the verbs, there is one conjugation for a male subject and another for a female subject. But these are straightforward to construct—take the verb stem of the infinitive verb and add a -ता, -ती, or -ते ending for male singular, female singular, or male plural forms, respectively.

Study the example shown below for जाना (jānā) *to go*.

Male singular:	*I go*	मैं जाता हूँ। (maiñ jātā huñ)
Female singular:	*I go*	मैं जाती हूँ। (maiñ jātī huñ)
Male singular:	*you (informal) go*	तू जाता है। (tū jātā hai)
Female singular:	*you (informal) go*	तू जाती है। (tū jātī hai)
Male singular:	*you (informal) go*	तुम जाते हो। (tum jāte ho)
Female singular:	*you (informal) go*	तुम जाती हो। (tum jātī ho)
Male singular:	*he/it goes*	यह/वह जाता है। (yah/vah jātā hai)
Female singular:	*she/it goes*	यह/वह जाती है। (yah/vah jātī hai)
Male honorary plural:	*you (formal) go*	आप जाते हैं। (āp jāte haiñ)
Female honorary plural:	*you (formal) go*	आप जाती हैं। (āp jātī haiñ)

Cultural note

For the purpose of conjugation, the formal *you* (आप) is treated as a plural. This concept in Hindi is called the "honorary" plural. It also applies to all subjects addressed with the respect marker जी.

Example: गीता जी जाती हैं। (Gītā jī jātī haiñ)		
Male plural:	*we go*	हम जाते हैं। (ham jāte haiñ)
Female plural:	*we go*	हम जाती हैं। (ham jātī haiñ)
Male plural:	*they/these/those go*	ये/वे जाते हैं। (ye/ve jāte haiñ)
Female plural:	*they/these/those go*	ये/वे जाती हैं। (ye/ve jātī haiñ)

EXERCISE

10·2

Conjugate the verb आना (ānā) *to come* in *the present indefinite form. (m. s. = male singular, m. pl. = male plural, f. s. = female singular, f. pl. = female plural). The conjugation for the verb to be is already provided.*

1. (*m. s.*): मैं _____ हूँ।
2. (*f. s.*): मैं _____ हूँ।
3. (*m. s.*): तू _____ है।
4. (*f. s.*): तू _____ है।
5. (*m. s.*): तुम _____ हो।
6. (*f. s.*): तुम _____ हो।
7. (*m. pl.*): आप _____ हैं।

8. (*f. pl.*): आप _____ हैं।
9. (*m. pl.*): हम _____ हैं।
10. (*f. pl.*): हम _____ हैं।
11. (*m. s.*): यह/वह _____ है।
12. (*f. s.*): यह/वह _____ है।
13. (*m. pl.*): ये/वे _____ हैं।
14. (*m. pl.*): ये/वे _____ हैं।

For the verb पढ़ना (paṛhnā): to read, study, *circle whether the present indefinite conjugation provided is correct or incorrect.*

1. (*m. s.*): मैं <u>पढ़ता</u> हूँ। Correct / Incorrect
2. (*f. s.*): मैं <u>पढ़ती</u> हूँ। Correct / Incorrect
3. (*m. s.*): तू <u>पढ़ता</u> है। Correct / Incorrect
4. (*f. s.*): तू <u>पढ़ती</u> है। Correct / Incorrect
5. (*m. s.*): तुम <u>पढ़ता</u> हो। Correct / Incorrect
6. (*f. s.*): तुम <u>पढ़ती</u> हो। Correct / Incorrect
7. (*m. pl.*): आप <u>पढ़ता</u> हैं। Correct / Incorrect
8. (*f. pl.*): आप <u>पढ़ता</u> हैं। Correct / Incorrect
9. (*m. pl.*): हम <u>पढ़ता</u> हैं। Correct / Incorrect
10. (*f. pl.*): हम <u>पढ़ता</u> हैं। Correct / Incorrect
11. (*m. s.*): यह/वह <u>पढ़ता</u> है। Correct / Incorrect
12. (*f. s.*): यह/वह <u>पढ़ती</u> है। Correct / Incorrect
13. (*m. pl.*): ये/वे <u>पढ़ती</u> हैं। Correct / Incorrect
14. (*f. pl.*): ये/वे <u>पढ़ती</u> हैं। Correct / Incorrect

More verbs • और क्रियाएँ

to buy	ख़रीदना (kharīdnā)	to understand	समझना (samajhnā)
to sell	बेचना (becnā)	to win	जीतना (jītnā)
to live	जीना (jīnā)	to lose	हारना (hārnā)
to die	मरना (marnā)	to walk	चलना (calnā)
to show	दिखाना (dikhānā)	to fly	उड़ना (uṛnā)

Conjugate the verbs and translate the following sentences into Hindi.

1. I (*male*) eat and drink. _____

2. She awakes. _____

3. They bathe. _____

4. You (formal) watch (see) TV (टी. वी.). _____

5. You (female) (informal) write. _____

6. They win. _____

7. We walk. _____

8. It flies. _____

Your daily routine • आपकी दिनचर्या

Daily routine • दिनचर्या

in the morning	सुबह (subah)	then	फिर (fir)
in the afternoon	दोपहर को (dopahar ko)	to watch TV	टी. वी. देखना (tī. vī. dekhnā)
in the evening	शाम को (śām ko)	to drive a car	गाड़ी चलाना (gāṛī calānā)
at night	रात को (rāt ko)	to work	काम करना (kām karnā)

Study the description of Ajay's daily routine.

मैं सुबह जागता हूँ। फिर, मैं नहाता हूँ। मैं गाड़ी चलाता हूँ। मैं खाता और पीता हूँ। दोपहर को, मैं पढ़ता हूँ, पर लिखता नहीं। शाम को, मैं टी. वी. देखता हूँ। फिर, काम करता हूँ और, रात को सोता हूँ।

Maiñ subah jāgtā huñ. Fir, maiñ nahātā huñ. Maiñ gāṛī calātā huñ. Maiñ khātā aur pītā huñ. Dopahar ko, maiñ paṛhtā huñ, par likhtā nahiñ. Śām ko, maiñ tī. vī. dekhtā huñ. Fir, kām kartā huñ aur, rāt ko, sotā huñ.

I wake up in the morning. Then, I bathe. I drive the car. I eat and drink. In the afternoon, I read, but don't write. In the evening, I watch TV. Then, I work and, at night, I sleep.

EXERCISE

10·5

Use the model above as a guide to help describe your typical daily routine.

_____

_____

_____

_____

_____

Numbers
संख्याएँ

Numbers 1–100 • १–१०० तक संख्याएँ

Here are the forms, spelling, and pronunciation of the Devnagari numerals.

1: १ एक (ek)	11: ११ ग्यारह (gyārah)	21: २१ इक्कीस (ikkīs)	31: ३१ इकतीस (ikattīs)	41: ४१ इकतालीस (iktālīs)
2: २ दो (do)	12: १२ बारह (bārah)	22: २२ बाईस (bāīs)	32: ३२ बत्तीस (battīs)	42: ४२ बयालीस (byālīs)
3: ३ तीन (tīn)	13: १३ तेरह (terah)	23: २३ तेईस (teīs)	33: ३३ तैंतीस (taiñtīs)	43: ४३ तैंतालीस (taiñtālīs)
4: ४ चार (cār)	14: १४ चौदह (caudah)	24: २४ चौबीस (caubīs)	34: ३४ चौंतीस (cauñtīs)	44: ४४ चवालीस (cavālīs)
5: ५ पाँच (pāñch)	15: १५ पंद्रह (paṇdrah)	25: २५ पच्चीस (paccīs)	35: ३५ पैंतीस (paiñtīs)	45: ४५ पैंतालीस (paiñtālīs)
6: ६ छ (che)	16: १६ सोलह (solah)	26: २६ छब्बीस (chabbīs)	36: ३६ छत्तीस (chattīs)	46: ४६ छियालीस (chiyālīs)
7: ७ सात (sāt)	17: १७ सत्रह (satrah)	27: २७ सत्ताईस (sattāīs)	37: ३७ सैंतीस (saiñtīs)	47: ४७ सैंतालीस (saiñtālīs)
8: ८ आठ (āṭh)	18: १८ अठारह (aṭhārah)	28: २८ अट्ठाईस (aṭṭhāīs)	38: ३८ अड़तीस (aṛtīs)	48: ४८ अड़तालीस (aṛtālīs)
9: ९ नौ (nau)	19: १९ उन्नीस (unnīs)	29: २९ उनतीस (untīs)	39: ३९ उनतालीस (untālīs)	49: ४९ उनचास (uncās)
10: १० दस (das)	20: २० बीस (bīs)	30: ३० तीस (tīs)	40: ४० चालीस (cālīs)	50: ५० पचास (pacās)

51: ५१ इक्यावन (ikyāvan)	61: ६१ इकसठ (iksaṭh)	71: ७१ इकहत्तर (ikhattar)	81: ८१ इक्यासी (ikyāsī)	91: ९१ इक्यानवे (ikyānave)
52: ५२ बावन (bāvan)	62: ६२ बासठ (bāsaṭh)	72: ७२ बहत्तर (bahattar)	82: ८२ बयासी (bayāsī)	92: ९२ बानवे (bānave)
53: ५३ तिरपन (tirpan)	63: ६३ तिरसठ (tirsaṭh)	73: ७३ तिहत्तर (tihattar)	83: ८३ तिरासी (tirāsī)	93: ९३ तिरानवे (tirānave)
54: ५४ चौवन (cauvan)	64: ६४ चौंसठ (cauñsaṭh)	74: ७४ चौहत्तर (cauhattar)	84: ८४ चौरासी (caurāsī)	94: ९४ चौरानवे (caurānave)
55: ५५ पचपन (pacpan)	65: ६५ पैंसठ (paiñsaṭh)	75: ७५ पचहत्तर (pacattar)	85: ८५ पचासी (pacāsī)	95: ९५ पचानवे (pacānave)
56: ५६ छप्पन (chappan)	66: ६६ छियासठ (chiyāsaṭh)	76: ७६ छिहत्तर (chihattar)	86: ८६ छियासी (chiyāsī)	96: ९६ छियानवे (chiyānave)
57: ५७ सत्तावन (sattāvan)	67: ६७ सरसठ (sarsaṭh)	77: ७७ सतहत्तर (sathattar)	87: ८७ सत्तासी (sattāsī)	97: ९७ सतानवे (sattānave)
58: ५८ अट्ठावन (aṭṭhāvan)	68: ६८ अड़सठ (aṛsaṭh)	78: ७८ अठहत्तर (aṭhhattar)	88: ८८ अट्ठासी (aṭṭhāsī)	98: ९८ अट्ठानवे (aṭṭhānave)
59: ५९ उनसठ (unsaṭh)	69: ६९ उनहत्तर (unhattar)	79: ७९ उन्यासी (unyāsī)	89: ८९ नवासी (navāsī)	99: ९९ निन्यानवे (ninyānave)
60: ६० साठ (sāṭh)	70: ७० सत्तर (sattar)	80: ८० अस्सी (assī)	90: ९० नब्बे (nabbe)	100: १०० सौ (sau)

0	शून्य (śūnya)
1000	एक हज़ार (ek hazār)
10,000	दस हज़ार (das hazār)
100,000	एक लाख (ek lākh)
1 million	दस लाख (das lākh)
10 million	एक करोड़ (ek karoṛ)
1 billion (American)	एक अरब (ek arab)
10,000 million	एक खरब (ek kharab)

Exchanging contact information • संपर्क की जानकारी का आदान-प्रदान

Cultural note

Most landline phone numbers in India are a maximum of ten digits and contain two or three digits of the Subscriber Trunk Dialing (STD) code and the number, written in the format STD-1234567. Mobile phone numbers vary based on the provider. Emergency phone numbers are usually of three digits: Police: 100, Fire: 101, Medical: 103.

आपका फ़ोन नम्बर क्या है? (āpkā fon namber kyā hai?)
What is your phone number?

मेरा फ़ोन नम्बर ११-९२५४०८८३१ है। (merā fon namber 11-925408831 hai.)
My phone number is 11-925408831. (11 is the STD code for New Delhi.)

आपका पता क्या है? (āpkā patā kyā hai?)
What is your address?

मेरा पता A-४ ब्लाक, पश्चिम विहार, नई दिल्ली ११००६३ है। (merā patā A-4 block, Paschim Vihar, New Delhi 110063 hai.)
My address is A-4 block, Paschim Vihar, New Delhi 110063.

अभ्यास
११·१

Practice asking and receiving contact information. Translate the Hindi phone numbers into English and provide a Hindi question that befits the answer provided in #3. And you'll notice that Hindi numerals are used to number exercises and questions from now on!

१. रमेश जी, आपका फ़ोन नम्बर क्या है?

मेरा फ़ोन नम्बर _____ है। (५२२-४२३७६५९८९)
शुक्रिया!

२. मीना जी, आपका फ़ोन नम्बर क्या है?

मेरा फ़ोन नम्बर _____ है। (२२-२१३६६४७०८)
शुक्रिया!

३. अमित जी, _____?

मेरा पता कमला नहरु कालेज, अगस्त क्रांति मार्ग, नई दिल्ली ११००४९ है।
शुक्रिया!

Today's date • आज की तारीख़

Cultural note

The format of dates in India starts with the date, then month, and ends with the year. For example: April 21, 2005 will be written as 21/4/05.

Conversationally, the word तारीख़ (tārīkh) is used for date and other words such as दिनांक (dināñk) and तिथि (tithi) are used in writing, as in newspapers or books.

What is the date today?

आज क्या तारीख़ है? (āj kyā tārīkh hai?) or

आज की तारीख़ क्या है? (āj kī tārīkh kyā hai?) or

इक्कीस जून (ikkis Jūn)

Note: Months in Hindi are given in the next chapter.

Age • आयु

Cultural note

In general, it is not considered rude to politely inquire about someone's age in India. It is not always viewed as private information, mostly because the idea of privacy is quite different in India. People in India are very friendly and will want to know more about you, including your age, and they will gladly reciprocate by volunteering their information.

Common words for *age*: उम्र (umar), आयु (āyu), and *year*: साल (sāl), वर्ष (varṣ).

Here are three ways of asking questions about age:

आपकी उम्र/आयु क्या है? (āpkī umar/āyu kyā hai?)	*What is your age?*
आपकी उम्र/आयु कितनी है? (āpkī umar/āyu kitnī hai?)	*How old are you?*
आप कितने साल के हैं? (āp kitne sāl ke haiñ?)	*How old are you?*

Examples:

आपकी उम्र क्या है? (āpkī umar kyā hai?)	*What is your age?*
मेरी उम्र २१ साल है। (merī umar ikkis sāl hai)	*I am 21 years old.*
मैं २१ साल का हूँ। (Male speaker: maiñ ikkis sāl kā huñ)	*I (male) 21 years old.*
मैं २१ साल की हूँ। (Female speaker: maiñ ikkis sāl kī huñ)	*I (female) am 21 years old.*
आपकी आयु कितनी है? (āpkī umar/āyu kitnī hai?)	*How old are you?*
मेरी आयु १९ वर्ष है। (merī āyu unnis varṣ hai)	*I am 19 years old.*
मैं १९ साल का हूँ। (Male speaker: maiñ unnis sāl kā huñ)	*I (male) am 19 years old.*
मैं १९ साल की हूँ। (Female speaker: maiñ unnis sāl kī huñ)	*I (female) am 19 years old.*
आप कितने साल के हैं? (āp kitne sāl ke haiñ?)	*How old are you?*
मैं ३० साल का हूँ। (Male speaker: maiñ tīs sāl kā huñ)	*I (male) am 30 years old.*
मैं ३० साल की हूँ। (Female speaker: maiñ tīs sāl kī huñ)	*I (female) am 30 years old.*

Note: The English translation of the sentences above is not literal, but represents the meaning of the Hindi sentences in English.

अभ्यास
११·२

Translate the following sentences into Hindi.

१. What is your phone number?   _____

२. My phone number is 11-423765989.   _____

३. What is the date today?   _____

४. Today is June 19th.   _____

५. How old are you?   _____

६. I (male) am 29 years old.   _____

७. What is your age?   _____

८. My age is 22 years.   _____

९. I (female) am 24 years old.   _____

अभ्यास
११·३

Integrate things you have learned so far and, using the model below, write a few sentences in Hindi talking about yourself. Use this model as a guide.

नमस्ते, मेरा नाम ज़ैक है। मैं अमरीकी हूँ और एक विद्यार्थी हूँ। मेरी उम्र १८ साल है। मैं हिन्दी पढ़ता हूँ। मैं हिन्दी पढ़ता और लिखता हूँ।

Namaste, merā nām Zack hai. Maiñ amrīkī huñ aur ek vidyārthī huñ. Merī umar 18 sāl hai. Maiñ Hindi paṛhtā huñ. Maiñ Hindi paṛhtā aur likhtā huñ.

Hello, My name is Zack. I am an American and a student. I am 18 years old. I study Hindi. I read and write Hindi.

_____

_____

_____

_____

_____

Possessives
संबंधकारक

Possessives • संबंधकारक

You have already encountered possessives in Hindi: मेरा नाम, आपका नाम, मेरी उम्र, etc. Each of the pronouns introduced before has three possessive forms—masculine singular, feminine, and masculine plural. Note that the feminine singular and plural are the same.

You will also notice that there is no difference between my and mine, your and yours, our and ours, etc. in Hindi. This is because the possessives already have the *'s* in them (postposition का, की, के, meaning *of*, or *'s* is addressed in greater detail in the following Part V, Chapter 15).

my/mine	मेरा (merā, *m. s.*), मेरी (merī, *f.*), मेरे (mere, *m. pl.*)
your/yours (informal)	तू: तेरा (terā, *m. s.*), तेरी (terī, *f.*), तेरे (tere, *m. pl.*)
your/yours (informal)	तुम्हारा (tumhārā, *m. s.*), तुम्हारी (tumhārī, *f.*), तुम्हारे (tumhāre, *m. pl.*)
your/yours (formal)	आपका (āpkā, *m. s.*), आपकी (āpkī, *f.*), आपके (āpke, *m. pl.*)
our/ours	हमारा (hamārā, *m. s.*), हमारी (hamārī, *f.*), हमारे (hamāre, *m. pl.*)
his/her/its (proximity)	इसका (iskā, *m. s.*), इसकी (iskī, *f.*), इसके (iske, *m. pl.*)
his/her/its (distance)	उसका (uskā, *m. s.*), उसकी (uskī, *f.*), उसके (uske, *m. pl.*)
their/theirs (proximity)	इनका (inkā, *m. s.*), इनकी (inkī, *f.*), इनके (inke, *m. pl.*)
their/theirs (distance)	उनका (unkā, *m. s.*), उनकी (unkī, *f.*), उनके (unke, *m. pl.*)

Write the possessive forms.

१. our/ours   _____

२. your/yours (*informal*)   _____

३. your/yours (*informal*)   _____

४. their/theirs (*proximity*)   _____

५. my/mine   _____

६. his/her/its (*proximity*)   _____

७. your/yours (*formal*)   _____

८. his/her/its (*distance*)   _____

९. their/theirs (*distance*)   _____

In Hindi, the possessive form is dependent on the gender and number of *what* is being owned or possessed; it is *not* determined by the gender and number of the owner(s).

For instance, with मेरा (*m.*), नाम (*m.*), मेरा (*m. s.*) is used regardless of whether the speaker is masculine or feminine; the masculine singular form of "my" is being used because नाम is masculine singular. As Hindi is a gendered language, each noun (person, place, or thing) has a gender and it is important to know how to make correct Hindi sentences.

Recall the names of objects in your room that you learned in Chapter 5 (Exercise 5.6). Here are their genders and numbers and here is how you can say that these objects are your/yours (mine):

किताब (*f. s.*)	book	मेरी किताब	*my book*
गिलास (*m. s.*)	drinking glass	मेरा गिलास	*my drinking glass*
जूते (*m. pl.*)	shoes	मेरे जूते	*my shoes*
कपड़े (*m. pl.*)	clothes	मेरे कपड़े	*my clothes*
एक लैपटाप (*m. s.*)	one laptop	मेरा लैपटाप	*my laptop*
दो मेज़ (*m. pl.*)	two tables	मेरे मेज़	*my tables*
क़लम (*f. s.*)	pen	मेरी क़लम	*my pen*
कुछ काग़ज़ (*m. pl.*)	some papers	मेरे काग़ज़	*my papers*
चाबी (*f. s.*)	key	मेरी चाबी	*my key*
पानी की बोतल (*f. s.*)	water bottle	मेरी पानी की बोतल	*my water bottle*

Use the possessive form and write the following items in Hindi.

१. your (*formal*) papers _____

२. his water bottle _____

३. your (*informal*) key _____

४. their clothes _____

५. his shoes _____

६. her shoes _____

७. your (*informal*) pen _____

८. their glass _____

९. our table _____

१०. your (*formal*) book _____

Use of possessives in sentences • संबंधकारक का वाक्यों में प्रयोग

Below is the structure of sentences with possessives, using किताब (*f. s.*) as an example.

This is my book.	यह मेरी किताब है।
This is your (formal) *book.*	यह आपकी किताब है।
This is your (informal) *book.*	यह तेरी किताब है।
This is your (informal) *book.*	यह तुम्हारी किताब है।
This is our book.	यह हमारी किताब है।
This is his/her book.	यह उसकी/इसकी किताब है।
This is their book.	यह उनकी/इनकी किताब है।

Write the following sentences in Hindi using the possessive.

१. This is my table. _____

२. This is your (*formal*) key. _____

३. This is your (*informal*) laptop. _____

४. This is your (*informal*) glass. _____

५. This is our water bottle. _____

६. This is his/her table. _____

७. This is their key. _____

Note: Sometimes there are variations in the sentence structure, depending on what is being emphasized. For instance, "this is *my* pen" would be यह <u>मेरी</u> क़लम है, "*this* is my pen" would be <u>यह</u> मेरी क़लम है, while "this pen is *mine*" would be यह क़लम <u>मेरी</u> है।

Mixed sentences • मिश्रित वाक्य

Enhance your understanding by studying these mixed sentences containing possessives that you just learned with other concepts such as nationalities, adding *and/but/both*, verbs, numbers, and *yes/no* questions that you learned before.

उनके लैपटाप जापानी हैं।	*Their laptops are Japanese.*
इनकी गाड़ी अमरीकी है।	*Their car is American.*
आप मेरी किताब पढ़ते हैं।	*You read my book.*
वह मेरा गिलास नहीं, आपका है।	*That is not my glass, (that) is your glass.*
क्या वे तीन काग़ज़ हमारे हैं?	*Are those three papers ours?*
जी नहीं, वे हमारे नहीं, उनके हैं।	*No, those are not ours, (those) are theirs.*
क्या यह क़लम तेरी है?	*Is this pen yours?*
हाँ, यह क़लम मेरी है।	*Yes, this pen is mine.*
ये दोनों गिलास मेरे हैं।	*These two glasses are mine.*
वे दोनों मेज़ उसके हैं।	*Those two tables are his/hers.*
ये दस जूते और काग़ज़ उसके हैं।	*These ten shoes and papers are his/hers.*
ये दस जूते उसके हैं, पर काग़ज़ हमारे हैं।	*These ten shoes are his/hers, but the papers are ours.*

Translate these sentences into Hindi.

१.   Their book is Greek.

_____

२.   Our table is Indian.

_____

३.   They read your (*formal*) book.

_____

४.   That is not his key, (that) is your (*formal*) key.

_____

५.   Are those my shoes?

_____

६.   No, those are not yours (*informal*), (those) are hers.

_____

७.   Is this laptop yours (*informal*)?

_____

८.   Yes, this laptop is mine, but that laptop is yours (*informal*).

_____

९.   These five glasses are mine.

_____

१०. That pen is his.

_____

११. These clothes are ours.

_____

१२. I drive your (*informal*) car.

_____

Reading practice • पढ़ने का अभ्यास

For added practice, read about Rajesh's (male) daily routine without transliteration.

राजेश की दिनचर्या

राजेश सुबह जल्दी उठता है। वह नहाता है और दाँत साफ़ करता है। फ़िर, वह नाश्ता बनाता है और खाता है। वह कपड़े पहनता है और दफ़्तर जाता है। वहाँ काम करता है। दोपहर को खाना खाता है। शाम को खरीदारी करता है और घर आता है। वह संगीत सुनता है और पत्रिका पढ़ता है। वह रात का खाना खाता है और फ़िर सोता है।

जल्दी (jaldī)	early
उठना (uṭhnā)	to get up
दाँत साफ़ करना (dãṅt sāf karna)	to brush one's teeth
फ़िर (fir)	then
नाश्ता बनाना (nāśtā banānā)	to make breakfast
कपड़े पहनना (kapṛe pahnanā)	to wear clothes
दफ़्तर (daftar)	office
वहाँ (vahãṅ)	over there
दोपहर को (dopahar ko)	in the afternoon
शाम को (śām ko)	in the evening
खरीदारी करना (kharīdārī karnā)	to shop
संगीत सुनना (saṅgīt sunanā)	to listen to music
पत्रिका पढ़ना (patrikā paṛhnā)	to read a magazine
रात का खाना (rāt kā khānā)	dinner

Based on the reading passage, answer these questions with a yes or no (जी हाँ/नहीं).

१. क्या राजेश शाम को उठता है? _____

२. क्या वह हिंदी पढ़ता है? _____

३. क्या राजेश सुबह संगीत सुनता है? _____

४. क्या वह दाँत साफ़ करता है? _____

५. क्या राजेश रात का खाना सुबह खाता है? _____

NOUNS
पाठ ५: संज्ञा

Grammar

Gender of persons
Postposition को
Postposition में
Gender of places
Postposition पर
Postposition से
Postposition तक
Number and gender of nouns
Possessives/postposition का

Vocabulary

Family
Days of the week
Months of the year
Places to go
Countries
Verbs with से
Parts of the day
Things around the house
Verbs with things in the house
Reading practice: Vocabulary

Culture

Addressing family members
Using Hindi and English months
Reading practice: Famous Indian celebrations

People
लोग

Gender of nouns: Persons • लिंग: व्यक्ति

In Hindi, every noun (person, place, or thing) has a gender. This is an important piece of information because the gender of every noun will determine which form (masculine or feminine) of the verb is used to convey the accurate message in a sentence.

As an example, below are commonly used kinship terms (nouns) in India and their genders, which correspond with the gender of the person, as one would expect.

Note that transliterations will no longer be regularly provided for new vocabulary and example sentences.

Relatives in an Indian family (kinship terms) • एक भारतीय परिवार के बंधु-जन

husband	पति (*m.*), शौहर (*m.*)	wife	पत्नी (*f.*), बीवी (*f.*)
father	पिता (*m.*), बाप (*m.*)	mother	माता (*f.*), माँ (*f.*)
male child	बच्चा (*m.*)	female child	बच्ची (*f.*)
son	बेटा (*m.*)/पुत्र (*m.*)	daughter	बेटी (*f.*)/पुत्री (*f.*)
brother	भाई/भैया (*m.*)	sister	बहन/बहिन (*f.*)
elder/younger brother	बड़ा/छोटा भाई (*m.*)	elder/younger sister	बड़ी/छोटी बहन (*f.*)
maternal grandfather	नाना (*m.*)	maternal grandmother	नानी (*f.*)
paternal grandfather	दादा (*m.*)	paternal grandmother	दादी (*f.*)
grandson (son's son)	पोता (*m.*)	granddaughter (son's daughter)	पोती (*f.*)

grandson (daughter's son)	नाती (m.)	granddaughter (daughter's daughter)	नातिन (f.)
son-in-law	दामाद (m.)	daughter-in-law	बहू (f.), पुत्रवधु (f.)
father-in-law	ससुर (m.)	mother-in-law	सास (f.)
brother-in-law (wife's brother)	साला (m.)	sister-in-law (wife's sister)	साली (f.)
brother-in-law (husband's elder brother)	जेठ (m.)	sister-in-law (his wife)	जेठानी (f.)
brother-in-law (husband's younger brother)	देवर (m.)	sister-in-law (his wife)	देवरानी (f.)
maternal uncle (mom's brother)	मामा (m.)	maternal aunt (his wife)	मामी (f.)
maternal uncle (mom's sister's husband)	मौसा (m.)	maternal aunt (mom's sister)	मौसी (f.)
paternal uncle (dad's elder brother)	ताऊ (m.)	paternal aunt (his wife)	ताई (f.)
paternal uncle (dad's younger brother)	चाचा (m.)	paternal aunt (his wife)	चाची (f.)
paternal uncle (dad's sister's husband)	फूफा (m.)	paternal aunt (dad's sister)	बुआ (f.)
nephew (sister's son)	भाँजा (m.)	niece (sister's daughter)	भाँजी (f.)
nephew (brother's son)	भतीजा (m.)	niece (brother's daughter)	भतीजी (f.)

Cultural insight

As this extensive network of kinship terms indicate, relationships and their maintainence play an integral role in Indian society. In addition, it is common practice for young people in India to refer to all types of actual uncles and aunts and older people unrelated to them generically as अंकल जी and आंटी जी. It is also a custom to address male strangers as भैया and female strangers as बहन जी. The word सगा, सगी, or सगे is used to refer to blood relatives and सौतेला, सौतेली, or सौतेले is used to refer to half/step relatives. Also, depending on the context, the term साला can be used as a derogatory word.

Match the corresponding masculine and feminine relatives.

M	F
१. पति	बहन/बहिन
२. पिता	नानी
३. बेटा/पुत्र	पत्नी
४. भाई/भैया	चाची
५. बड़ा/छोटा भाई	दादी
६. नाना	सास
७. दादा	मामी
८. ससुर	बेटी/पुत्री
९. मामा	मौसी
१०. मौसा	बड़ी/छोटी बहन
११. चाचा	माता

In this exercise, Anil is talking about his family. Note the possessives and honorary plurals used with the kinship terms. Fill in the blanks with the kinship terms.

मैं अनिल हूँ और यह मेरा परिवार (family) है।

१. मेरे _____ (father) जी अध्यापक हैं।

२. मेरी _____ (mother) जी वक़ील हैं।

३. मेरा _____ (elder brother) चिकित्सक है।

४. मेरा _____ (younger brother) कलाकार है।

५. मेरी _____ (elder sister) नर्स हैं।

६. मेरी _____ (younger sister) अभिनेत्री है।

Babita is talking about her family. Fill in the missing words.

मेरे (१.) _____ (husband) अमरीकन हैं, पर मैं इतालवी हूँ। मेरा (२.) _____ (son) और (३.) _____ (daughter) दोनों अमरीकन हैं। उनकी उम्र १८ साल है। वे पढ़ते हैं। मेरे (४.) _____ (maternal grandfather) जी सेवानिवृत (retired) हैं, पर मेरी (५.) _____ (maternal grandmother) जी काम करती हैं।

Postposition को with days of the week • हफ़्ते/सप्ताह के दिन

What is known as a *preposition* (*to, in*, etc.) in English is a *post*position in Hindi. This is because in Hindi, *to, in*, etc. are placed *after* the noun. For example, को is a postposition meaning *to*. If you want to say "to you (formal)" in Hindi, you will say आप को. Uses of को will be explained in upcoming chapters. Sometimes, however, the postposition को will also have other uses that are not similar to the uses in English. For example, को is commonly used with days of the week. To say that something happened *on Monday*, one would say <u>सोमवार</u> (*somvār: Monday*) <u>को</u>.

Monday	सोमवार (somvār)
Tuesday	मंगलवार (mañgalvār)
Wednesday	बुधवार (budhvār)
Thursday	गुरुवार (guruvār), बृहस्पतिवार (brihaspativār)
Friday	शुक्रवार (śukravār)
Saturday	शनिवार (śanivār), शनीचर (śanīcar)
Sunday	रविवार (ravivār), इतवार (itvār)

Note: To say that something happened *on Mondays* or *on a Monday*, one would also translate as <u>सोमवार को</u>.

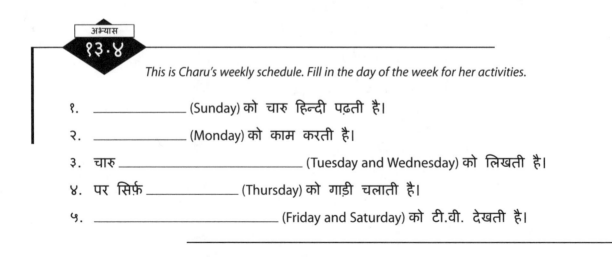

This is Charu's weekly schedule. Fill in the day of the week for her activities.

१. _____ (Sunday) को चारु हिन्दी पढ़ती है।

२. _____ (Monday) को काम करती है।

३. चारु _____ (Tuesday and Wednesday) को लिखती है।

४. पर सिर्फ़ _____ (Thursday) को गाड़ी चलाती है।

५. _____ (Friday and Saturday) को टी.वी. देखती है।

Postposition में with months of the year • साल के महीने

Postposition में means *in*, *into*, and *inside* and, similar to को, it is placed after the noun. For instance, if you wanted to say *in October*, you would say अक्तूबर में (Aktūbar mein).

> ## Cultural note
>
> Hindi speakers use both Hindi months and English months in Hindi. Hindi months are more prevalent in religious Hindu contexts, such as fairs, festivals, and rituals, while Anglicized months in Hindi are used for all matters.
>
> ### Anglicized months in Hindi
>
> | | | | |
> |---|---|---|---|
> | January | जनवरी | July | जुलाई |
> | February | फ़रवरी | August | अगस्त |
> | March | मार्च | September | सितम्बर |
> | April | अप्रैल | October | अक्तूबर |
> | May | मई | November | नवम्बर |
> | June | जून | December | दिसम्बर |

Asking about birthdays • जन्मदिन के बारे में पूछना

birthday	जन्मदिन (*m.*)
month	महीना (*m.*)

In which month does your birthday occur?
आपका जन्मदिन किस महीने में होता है? (āpkā janamdin kis mahīne maiñ hotā hai?)

My birthday occurs in July.
मेरा जन्मदिन जुलाई में होता है। (merā janamdin julāī maiñ hotā hai)

In which month is your mom's birthday?
आपकी माता जी का जन्मदिन किस महीने में है?
(āpkī mātājī kā janamdin kis mahīne maiñ hai?)

In January.
जनवरी में।

अभ्यास
१३·५

Translate the answers to the following questions.

१. Q. आपका जन्मदिन किस महीने में होता है?

   A. _____ (My birthday occurs in December.)

२. Q. आपकी बहन का जन्मदिन किस महीने में है?

   A. _____ (My sister's birthday is in February.)

३. Q. आज क्या तारीख़ है?

   A. _____ (Today's date is May 2nd.)

·14·

Places
स्थान

Gender of nouns: Places • लिंग: स्थान

The names of places in Hindi tend to be masculine because they fit the two main types of nouns that are generally marked as masculine—the nouns that end with a consonant and the nouns that end with the vowel आ.

Places generally require the postpositions में (*in*) or पर (*at/on*). (Note: पर has two meanings; one as *but* that you encountered before and another as a postposition *at/on*, depending on the context.)

Places to go • जाने के स्थान

airport	हवाई अड्डा
bank	बैंक
beach	समुद्र तट, समुद्र का किनारा
bus stop	बस स्टैंड
city	शहर
college	महाविद्यालय, कालेज
garden	बाग, बगीचा
heaven	स्वर्ग, जन्नत
hell	नरक, जहन्नुम
historical building	एतिहासिक इमारत
home	घर
hospital	अस्पताल, चिकित्सालय
hostel/dormitory	छात्रावास
hotel/motel	होटल
houses of worship	
church	गिरजाघर
temple	मंदिर
mosque	मस्जिद
Sikh temple	गुरुद्वारा

library	पुस्तकालय
market	बाज़ार
monument	स्मारक
movie theater	सिनेमाघर
museum	संग्रहालय
national park	राष्ट्रीय उद्यान
office	दफ़्तर
outside	बाहर
pharmacy	दवाखाना
place	जगह
police station	पुलिस स्टेशन
post office	डाकघर
restaurant	भोजनालय, रेस्तरां (रैसटोरैंट)
school	विद्यालय, स्कूल
toilet (other than at home)	शौचालय
train station	रेलवे स्टेशन
university	विश्वविद्यालय
village	गाँव
zoo	चिड़ियाघर

Some useful verbs

to reside/stay	रहना
to roam	घूमना
to stroll	सैर करना, टहलना
to pray	पूजा करना
to wait	इंतज़ार करना

The verb *to go* (जाना) is really *to go to* in Hindi. This means that a Hindi postposition, corresponding to the last *to* in English, is not required.

हम दोनों चिड़ियाघर जाते हैं।	*We both go to the zoo.*
मीना और शालु बाज़ार जाते हैं।	*Meena and Shalu go to the market.*
तुम सिनेमाघर जाते हो।	*You go to the movie theater.*
वह सोमवार को पुलिस स्टेशन और बैंक जाता है।	*He goes to the police station and the bank on Monday.*
मैं घर जाती हूँ।	*I go home.*

Using postposition में

When talking about an activity in a particular place, especially in a building or an enclosed area, में is used after the name of the place.

मैं विद्यालय में पढ़ता हूँ।	*I study in school.*
वह बाग में सैर करता है।	*He strolls in the garden.*
यह भोजनालय में खाती है।	*She eats in/at the restaurant.*
मीना और शालु बाज़ार में घूमते हैं।	*Meena and Shalu roam in the market.*
आप होटल में सोते हैं।	*You sleep in a hotel.*
तुम सिनेमाघर में फ़िल्म देखते हो।	*You watch a movie in a movie theater.*
ये मंदिर में पूजा करते हैं।	*They worship in the temple.*
मैं घर में रहती हूँ।	*I live in a house.*

Using postposition पर

When talking about an activity in an open or a large area or an abstract location, पर is used after the noun.

Open areas

वे समुद्र तट पर घूमते हैं।	*They roam at the beach.*
मैं रेलवे स्टेशन पर हूँ।	*I am at the railway station.*
वह बस स्टैंड पर इंतज़ार करता है।	*He waits at the bus stop.*

Abstract locations

मैं घर पर हूँ।	*I am at home.*
मैं समय पर दफ़्तर जाता हूँ।	*I go to the office on time.*
मैं काम पर जाता हूँ।	*I go to work.*

अभ्यास
१४·१

Phalguni is talking about her sister's weekly activities. Fill out the missing information in Hindi.

१. सोमवार को मेरी बहन _____ (goes to the university).

२. मंगलवार को वह _____ (works in a hospital).

३. बुधवार को _____ (goes to the post office).

४. गुरुवार को _____ (goes to the movie theater).

५. शुक्रवार को _____ (stays at home).

६. शनिवार को _____ (eats at the restaurant).

७. रविवार को _____ (prays at the church).

Match the object or person with the respective location.

१.	विद्यार्थी	चिड़ियाघर
२.	अध्यापक	बाज़ार
३.	बावरची (cook/chef)	विद्यालय
४.	चिकित्सक	बाग
५.	माली	चिकित्सालय
६.	शेर (lion)	छात्रावास
७.	विक्रेता	भोजनालय
८.	हवाई जहाज़ (airplane)	गिरजाघर
९.	डाकिया	गुरुद्वारा
१०.	खज़ाँची	मस्जिद
११.	ईसाई (Christian)	हवाई अड्डा
१२.	हिंदु (Hindu)	मंदिर
१३.	सिख (Sikh)	डाकघर
१४.	मुसलमान (Muslim)	बैंक

Postposition से: Countries and verbs • देश व क्रियाएँ

The postposition से means *from, by, with,* or *since*. In addition to its use with certain verbs, it is commonly used with countries.

आप कहाँ से हैं?	*Where are you from?*
मैं अमरीका से हूँ।	*I am from America.*
वह स्वीडन से है।	*S/He is from Sweden.*
आपका दोस्त मिस्र से है।	*Your friend is from Egypt.*
मेरी नानी भारत से है।	*My grandma is from India.*

कहाँ	where
दोस्त, मित्र, सहेली	friend, gal pal

Write these sentences in Hindi using the postposition से.

१. We are from Japan (जापान). _____

२. But they are from China (चीन). _____

३. Both are from India. _____

४. You (*formal*) are from Greece (यूनान). _____

५. You (*informal*) are from Africa (अफ़्रीका). _____

६. Frank (फ्रैंक) is from Europe (यूरोप). _____

७. Radha (राधा) is from Canada (कैनेडा). _____

John is telling us about his friend Marc.

मेरा दोस्त मार्क फ़्राँस से है। वह बीस साल का है। वह स्कूल में पढ़ता है। सोमवार से शुक्रवार वह सिनेमाघर में काम करता है। शनिवार और रविवार को वह संग्रहालय जाता है।

Using this paragraph as a model, write a few things in Hindi about a friend of yours.

My friend Mark is from France. His age is Twenty year.
He study in school. Monday to Friday He is work to
Movie theather, saturday & Sunday he go to
Library.

Verbs with से

Many verbs in Hindi take postpositions. Here are some common verbs that require से because the activity is *from, by,* or *with* someone:

to love	से प्यार करना
to marry	से शादी करना
to ask	से पूछना
to say	से कहना
to talk	से बात करना
to argue	से बहस करना
to shake hands	से हाथ मिलाना

to be scared	से डरना
to be angry	से नाराज़ होना
to fight	से लड़ना

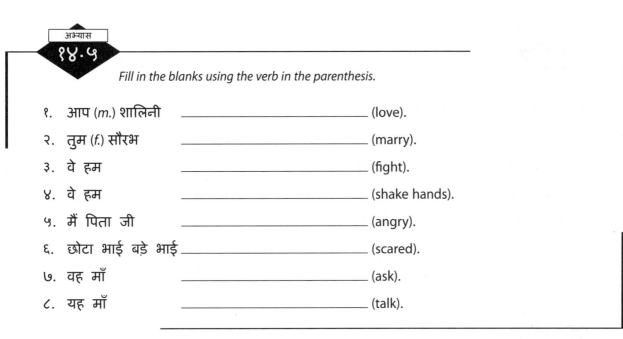

अभ्यास
१४·५

Fill in the blanks using the verb in the parenthesis.

१. आप (*m.*) शालिनी _____ (love).

२. तुम (*f.*) सौरभ _____ (marry).

३. वे हम _____ (fight).

४. वे हम _____ (shake hands).

५. मैं पिता जी _____ (angry).

६. छोटा भाई बड़े भाई _____ (scared).

७. वह माँ _____ (ask).

८. यह माँ _____ (talk).

Postposition तक with parts of the day • दिन के भाग

Postposition तक means *till*, *until*, or *up to*, and, similar to other basic Hindi postpositions introduced in this chapter, it is placed after the time or location. For example, *until Tuesday* is मंगलवार तक.

वह दिसम्बर तक दिल्ली में रहता है।	*He stays in Delhi till December.*
क्या आप शुक्रवार तक काम करते हैं?	*Do you work till Friday?*
यह रास्ता कहाँ तक जाता है?	*(Until) how far does this way/route go?*
यह रास्ता संग्रहालय तक जाता है।	*This way/route goes till the museum.*

The time of day • दिन के समय

morning	सुबह
afternoon	दोपहर
evening	शाम
night	रात
midnight	आधी रात
today	आज
tomorrow	कल
yesterday	कल
day after tomorrow	परसों
every day	हर रोज़

वह सुबह तक सोता है।   He sleeps until the morning.

शाम तक हम घर नहीं आते।   We don't come home till the evening.

वे आधी रात तक फ़िल्म देखते हैं।   They watch films until midnight.

Circle whether the location of the postposition तक is correct or incorrect in these sentences.

१. वह काम से घर तक गाड़ी चलाता है।   Incorrect / Correct

२. तक हम सुबह से शाम पढ़ते हैं।   Incorrect / Correct

३. शनिवार से तक रविवार गीता घूमती है।   Incorrect / Correct

४. जनवरी तक वे पोलैंड में रहते हैं।   Incorrect / Correct

५. मनीश हर रोज़ मंदिर जाता तक है।   Incorrect / Correct

Fill in the blanks with the appropriate postposition: को, में, पर, से, *or* तक.

१. रमेश बैंक _____ काम करता है।

२. हम रविवार _____ दिल्ली जाते है।

३. क्या आपका जन्मदिन फ़रवरी _____ है?

४. वे समुद्र तट _____ टहलते हैं।

५. मैं छात्रावास _____ रहता हूँ।

६. जेकब रूस _____ है।

७. उसकी माता जी जर्मनी _____ हैं।

८. यह रेलवे स्टेशन _____ इंतज़ार करता है।

९. हम सुबह _____ सोते हैं।

१०. वे जुलाई _____ भारत जाते हैं।

११. क्या तुम राष्ट्रीय उद्यान _____ घूमते हो?

१२. वह बुधवार _____ मंदिर जाता है।

Around the house
घर के आसपास

Number and gender of nouns • वचन और लिंग

You have seen in the previous chapters that all nouns (persons, places, and things) have a gender in Hindi that needs to be memorized for correct conjugation. Although there are several exceptions to this general rule, as a memory aide, it is still helpful to remember that nouns that end with a consonant or the diacritic mark for आ tend to be masculine and nouns that end with ई or its diacritic mark tend to be feminine. This general rule will also apply when changing a singular noun to a plural noun.

- ◆ Masculine plurals
  1. Masculine singular nouns that end with a consonant, such as अध्यापक, पुत्र, or चिड़ियाघर, stay the same in the plural form. Context indicates that the noun is plural.

  2. Masculine singular nouns that end with the diacritic mark for आ, such as बेटा, हवाई अड्डा, or बगीचा, are pluralized by changing the diacritic mark for आ to ए. For example, बेटा becomes बेटे (*sons*), हवाई अड्डा changes to हवाई अड्डे (*airports*), and बगीचा becomes बगीचे (*gardens*).

  3. Certain masculine singular nouns that end with the diacritic mark for आ, such as पिता, रेस्तरां, or विक्रेता, stay the same in the plural form. You will learn the most common examples later.

  4. Masculine singular nouns that end with other vowels (aside from आ) such as भाई, पति, or ताऊ also stay the same in the plural form.

- ◆ Feminine plurals
  1. Feminine singular nouns that end with a consonant, such as किताब, बहन, or रात, are pluralized by adding the diacritic mark for ए and a nasal dot. For example, किताब becomes किताबें (*books*), बहन turns into बहनें (*sisters*), and रात becomes रातें (*nights*).

  2. Feminine singular nouns that end with vowel आ, such as माता, are changed into a plural form by adding the diacritic mark for ए and the additional nasal Candra bindu. For example, माता becomes माताएँ (*mothers*).

  3. Similarly, feminine singular nouns that end with the long vowel ऊ or ई, such as बहू, बेटी, or अभिनेत्री, are changed into plural forms by shortening the vowel and adding the suffix -याँ. For example, बहू becomes बहुएँ (*daughter-in-laws*), बेटी turns into बेटियाँ (*daughters*), and अभिनेत्री changes to अभिनेत्रियाँ (*actresses*).

  4. Feminine singular nouns that already have a shortened vowel and end with a या, such as चिड़िया (*sparrow*) or गुड़िया (*doll*), are pluralized by adding the Candra bindu. For example, चिड़िया would become चिड़ियाँ and गुड़िया would be गुड़ियाँ.

Remember, the key to changing the masculine or feminine singular to its correct plural is first knowing whether the noun is masculine or feminine and then identifying how its type changes.

अभ्यास
१५·१

Change these masculine singular nouns into plural after दो (two).

१. एक संग्रहालय, दो _____

२. एक बैंक, दो _____

३. एक लेखक, दो _____

४. एक घर, दो _____

५. एक पिता, दो _____

६. एक अभिनेता, दो _____

७. एक अभियंता, दो _____

८. एक विक्रेता, दो _____

९. एक बेटा, दो _____

१०. एक बस अड्डा, दो _____

११. एक बगीचा, दो _____

१२. एक पोता, दो _____

१३. एक पति, दो _____

१४. एक भाई, दो _____

१५. एक दर्जी, दो _____

१६. एक ताऊ, दो _____

अभ्यास
१५·२

Change these feminine singular nouns into plural.

१. एक क़लम, दो _____

२. एक बहन, दो _____

३. एक क़िताब, दो _____

४. एक रात, दो _____

५. एक माता, दो _____

६. एक गायिका, दो _____

७. एक बुआ, दो _____

८. एक लेखिका, दो _____

९. एक चाबी, दो _____

१०. एक बेटी, दो _____

११. एक अभिनेत्री, दो _____

१२. एक चिड़िया, दो _____

१३. एक गुड़िया, दो _____

१४. एक बिटिया, दो _____

Convert these masculine and feminine singular nouns into plural.

१. एक गिरजाघर, दो _____

२. एक बिटिया, दो _____

३. एक अभियंता, दो _____

४. एक काग़ज़, दो _____

५. एक चाची, दो _____

६. एक बहू, दो _____

७. एक हवाई अड्डा, दो _____

८. एक माता, दो _____

९. एक खज़ाँची, दो _____

Number and gender of nouns: Things in the house • वचन और लिंग: घर में वस्तुएँ

Parts of the house • घर के हिस्से

bathroom	स्नानघर (*m.*), गुसलखाना (*m.*)	garden/yard	बगीचा (*m.*)
bedroom	शयन कक्ष (*m.*), सोने का कमरा (*m.*)	kitchen	रसोई (*f.*)
courtyard	आंगन (*m.*)	living room	बैठक (*m.*)
deck	चबूतरा (*m.*)	porch	द्वारमंडप (*m.*)
driveway	ड्राईव वे (*m.*)	room	कमरा (*m.*)
garage	गैराज (*m.*)		

Inside the house • घर के अंदर

Eating and drinking • खाना व पीना

basket	टोकरी (f.)	kitchen knife	चाकू (m.)
bowl, dish	कटोरी (f.)	knife	छुरी (f.)
carved earthen or metal pitcher with a long spout	सुराही (f.)	plate, platter	थाली (f.), प्लेट (f.)
dish, eating utensil	बर्तन (m.)	spatula, serving spoon	कड़छी (f.)
drinking glass	गिलास (m.)	spoon	चम्मच (m.)
earthen water pitcher with decoration	घड़ा (m.), मटका (m.)	strainer	छलनी (f.)
fork	कांटा (m.)		

Sleeping • सोना

bed sheet	चादर (f.)	closet or cabinet	अलमारी (f.)
bed	पलंग (m.), चारपाई (f.)	mattress	तलाई (f.), गद्दा (m.)
bedding	बिस्तर (m.)	pillow	तकिया (m.)
blanket (fleece or otherwise)	कंबल (m.)	quilt, duvet, comforter	रजाई (f.)

In the house • घर में

carpet, large rug	कालीन (m.)	light	बत्ती (f.), लाईट (f.)
ceiling or table fan	पंखा (m.)	picture, photo, poster, painting	तस्वीर (f.), चित्र (m.)
chair	कुर्सी (f.)	roof, ceiling	छत (f.)
couch, sofa	सोफ़ा (m.)	small rug	दरी (f.)
curtain	पर्दा (m.)	stairs	सीढ़ियाँ (f. pl.)
door	दरवाज़ा (m.)	TV	टी. वी. (m.)
doorbell	घंटी (f.)	table	मेज़ (m. & f.)
doormat	पायदान (m.)	vase	फूलदान (m.)
floor	फ़र्श (m.)	wall	दीवार (f.)
lamp	लैंप (f.)	window	खिड़की (f.)

Bathing • नहाना

faucet, tap	नल (m.)	toothpaste	टूथपेस्ट (f.)
soap	साबुन (m.)	towel	तौलिया (m.)
tooth brushing powder	मंजन (m.)	trash, garbage can	कूड़ेदान (m.)
toothbrush	टूथब्रश (m.)		

General houseware • सामान्य घर की चीज़ें

matchbox	माचिस की डिब्बी (*f.*)	mirror	शीशा (*m.*), आईना (*m.*)
matchstick	तीली (*f.*)	mop	पोछा (*m.*)
broom	झाड़ू (*m.*)	scissors	कैंची (*f.*)
bucket	बाल्टी (*f.*)	umbrella	छतरी (*f.*), छाता (*m.*)
candle	मोमबत्ती (*f.*)		

Outside the house • बाहर

flower pot	गमला (*m.*)	leaf	पत्ता (*m.*)
flower	फूल (*m.*)	plant	पौधा (*m.*)
fountain	फ़व्वारा (*m.*)	shrub, bush, hedge	झाड़ी (*f.*)
grass	घास (*f.*)	tree	पेड़ (*m.*)
ground	ज़मीन (*f.*)		

अभ्यास १५·४

Circle the correct plural of these singular nouns.

१.	दरवाज़ा	दरवाज़ा or दरवाज़े
२.	घंटी	घंटी or घंटियाँ
३.	पायदान	पायदान or पायदाने
४.	सीढ़ी	सीढ़ी or सीढ़ियाँ
५.	खिड़की	खिड़की or खिड़कियाँ
६.	कालीन	कालीन or कालीने
७.	दरी	दरी or दरियाँ
८.	पंखा	पंखा or पंखे
९.	दीवार	दीवार or दीवारें
१०.	तस्वीर	तस्वीर or तस्वीरें
११.	चित्र	चित्र or चित्रे
१२.	अलमारी	अलमारी or अलमारियाँ
१३.	कुर्सी	कुर्सी or कुर्सियाँ
१४.	टी. वी.	टी. वी. or टी. वियाँ
१५.	छुरी	छुरी or छुरियाँ
१६.	कांटा	कांटा or कांटे

१७.	चम्मच	चम्मच or चम्मचे
१८.	गिलास	गिलास or गिलासे
१९.	थाली	थाली or थालियाँ
२०.	पलंग	पलंग or पलंगे
२१.	बिस्तर	बिस्तर or बिस्तरियाँ
२२.	तकिया	तकिया or तकिए
२३.	रजाई	रजाई or रजाइयाँ
२४.	कंबल	कंबल or कंबले
२५.	चादर	चादर or चादरें
२६.	पर्दा	पर्दा or पर्दे
२७.	शीशा	शीशा or शीशे
२८.	नल	नल or नले
२९.	साबुन	साबुन or साबुने
३०.	तौलिया	तौलिया or तौलिए
३१.	पेड़	पेड़ or पेड़े
३२.	पौधा	पौधा or पौधे
३३.	झाड़ी	झाड़ी or झाड़ियाँ
३४.	फूल	फूल or फूले
३५.	फ़व्वारा	फ़व्वारा or फ़व्वारे
३६.	गमला	गमला or गमले

What is in your room? • आपके कमरे में क्या-क्या है?

In the following conversation, Sadhna is telling Jyoti about the things that are in her room.

ज्योतिः साधना जी, आपके कमरे में क्या-क्या है?

साधनाः मेरे कमरे में एक पलंग है और दो लैंप हैं। दोनों लैंप इतालवी हैं। मेज़ पर लैपटाप है, पर क़लम नहीं है। दो कुर्सियाँ हैं। छत पर पंखा है। फ़र्श पर कालीन है। ज़मीन पर तीन पौधे हैं। एक दीवार पर तस्वीर है। एक अलमारी है। अलमारी में किताबें हैं। दो खिड़कियाँ हैं। एक खिड़की पर पर्दा है। टी.वी. नहीं है।

अभ्यास १५.५

Using the conversation above as a model, describe in Hindi some of the things that are in your home.

_____

_____

_____

_____

_____

_____

_____

_____

अभ्यास १५.६

क्या कहाँ है? (What is where?)

Use the chart below to place each item in the part of the house where it is likely to be found.

चित्र, कालीन, कंबल, मेज़, छुरी, शीशा, तकिया, तौलिया, कूड़ेदान, थाली, गद्दा, लैंप, कांटा, साबुन, प्लेट, झाड़ू, झाड़ी, पर्दा, बर्तन, नल, अलमारी, सोफ़ा, गिलास, गमला, फूल, फूलदान, फव्वारा, पलंग, टी.वी., टूथब्रश, टूथपेस्ट, बिस्तर, आईना, पंखा, पौधा, पेड़, पोछा, चादर, रजाई, पत्ता, गाड़ी

बैठक	रसोई	शयन कक्ष	स्नानघर	बगीचा	गैराज

◆16◆ More verbs and possessives
अधिक क्रियाएँ व संबंधकारक

Verbs used with household objects • घर की वस्तुओं के साथ प्रयोग होने वाली क्रियाएँ

Here are some new verbs that are used with everyday objects in the house. An example of usage in the present tense is also shown.

to sit बैठना
नाना जी बैठक में कुर्सी पर <u>बैठते</u> हैं। वे टी. वी. देखते हैं।
Grandpa sits on a chair. He watches TV.

to cook खाना पकाना
(As a noun, खाना means *food* and as a verb, it means *to eat*.)
माँ रसोई में <u>खाना पकाती</u> हैं।
Mom cooks in the kitchen.

to put something (like a blanket) over oneself ओढ़ना
लोग रजाई या कंबल <u>ओढ़ते</u> हैं।
People put over (themselves) a quilt or a blanket.

to use इस्तेमाल करना
हम स्नानघर में <u>नहाते</u> हैं। तौलिया, साबुन, टूथब्रश, व टूथपेस्ट <u>इस्तेमाल करते</u> हैं। शीशा या आईना देखते हैं।
We take a shower/bath in the bathroom. Use a towel, soap, toothbrush, and toothpaste. Look in the mirror or looking glass.

to keep, put रखना
पिता जी गैराज में गाड़ी <u>रखते</u> हैं।
Father keeps the car in the garage.

to ring, to play (an instrument) बजाना
लोग घंटी <u>बजाते</u> हैं।
People ring a bell.

to clean साफ़ करना
वे पायदान पर जूते <u>साफ़ करते</u> हैं।
They clean (off) their shoes on the doormat.

to walk चलना
ये फ़र्श पर <u>चलते</u> हैं।
They walk on the floor.

to apply or affix something लगाना
आप फ़र्श पर झाड़ू और पोछा <u>लगाते</u> हैं।
You sweep and mop the floor.

to spread out something for use (e.g., bed sheet) बिछाना
लोग चादर, कालीन, और दरी <u>बिछाते</u> हैं।
People spread out a bed sheet, a big rug, and a small rug.

And here are some more common household-related verbs.

to pick up something/someone उठाना
फिर, चादर, कालीन, और दरी <u>उठाते</u> हैं।
Then, (people) pick up the bed sheet, big rug, and small rug.

to start, turn on, run something चलाना
पंखा, नल, और फव्वारा <u>चलाते</u> हैं। फिर, बंद करते हैं।
A fan, a faucet, and a fountain are turned on. Then, they are turned off.

to hang something टाँगना
विक्रम जी दीवार पर तस्वीरें या चित्र <u>टाँगते</u> हैं।
Vikram Ji hangs pictures or paintings on the wall.

to put, to pour something डालना
माली फूलदान में फूल <u>डालता</u> है। बावरची कड़छी से खाना प्लेट में <u>डालता</u> है।
The gardener puts flowers in the vase. The cook puts food on the plate with a serving spoon.

to take something out निकालना
फिर, हम फूलदान से फूल <u>निकालते</u> हैं।
Then, we take flowers out of the vase.

to turn on something (e.g., a light), to burn जलाना
लोग लैंप, बत्ती, और माचिस की तीली <u>जलाते</u> हैं।
People turn on a lamp, a light, and (light) a matchstick.

to turn something (containing light) off बुझाना
रात को तुम लैंप, बत्ती, और माचिस की तीली <u>बुझाते</u> हो।
At night, you turn off the lamp, light, and matchstick.

to fill something भरना
वे बाल्टी में पानी <u>भरते</u> हैं।
They fill the bucket with water. (In Hindi: fill the water in the bucket.)

to throw फेंकना
हम कूड़ेदान में कूड़ा <u>फेंकते</u> हैं।
We throw trash in the trash can.

Complete the following sentences using the appropriate verb.

१. जोसफ़ पंखा _____

२. हम रसोई में खाना _____

३. वे दोनों दरवाज़ा _____

४. आप घंटी _____

५. साहिल कूड़ा _____

६. यह पायदान पर जूते _____

७. रोहित फ़र्श पर _____

८. शोभा दीवार पर तस्वीरें _____

९. क्या तुम फूलदान में फूल _____

१०. पिता जी कुर्सी पर _____

११. माता जी लैंप _____

१२. छोटी बहन दरी _____

१३. बड़ा भाई झाड़ू _____

१४. नानी जी रजाई _____

१५. नवीन बाग में _____

Postposition का with possessives and more • संबंधकारक

The postposition **का** means "*of and 's.*" You have already seen this postposition in use several times in the earlier chapters. Recall the possessives आपका, इसका, उसका, इनका, and उनका. These possessives have the postposition **का** after the pronoun to indicate "*of or 's.*" Forms such as मेरा, हमारा, तुम्हारा, and तेरा are simply the combination of the pronoun and the postposition— मैं + का = मेरा, हम + का = हमारा, तुम + का = तुम्हारा, and तू + का = तेरा.

Recall also that all the possessives have the masculine singular, feminine singular/plural, and masculine plural versions. Let's review:

	(m. s.)	(f. s./f. pl.)	(m. pl.)
my/mine	मेरा	मेरी	मेरे
your/yours (informal)	तेरा	तेरी	तेरे
your/yours (informal)	तुम्हारा	तुम्हारी	तुम्हारे
your/yours (formal)	आपका	आपकी	आपके
our/ours	हमारा	हमारी	हमारे
his/her/its (proximity)	इसका	इसकी	इसके
his/her/its (distance)	उसका	उसकी	उसके
their/theirs (proximity)	इनका	इनकी	इनके
their/theirs (distance)	उनका	उनकी	उनके

As can be seen in the possessives, the postposition का has three forms: का (*m. s.*), की (*f. s./f. pl.*), and के (*m. pl.*). The only difference with using this postposition with nouns is that the postposition is not combined in written form. For example, if you wanted to say *Sean's*, you would say <u>शान का</u> (with a space before the postposition), not शानका.

अमित का भाई	Amit's brother
वसुधा की बहन	Vasudha's sister
सोनल का चाचा	Sonal's paternal uncle
यशु की किताब	Yashu's book
दीपक का मेज़	Deepak's table
प्रशांत का लैपटाप	Prashant's laptop

EXERCISE
१६·२

Write the following phrases in Hindi.

१. Dan's TV _____

२. Carla's fan _____

३. Bob's small rug _____

४. Ian's shoes _____

५. Samantha's house _____

६. Al's dad _____

७. Gavin's mom _____

८. Harry's sister _____

९. Sabrina's brother _____

१०. Chris' car _____

Reading practice • पढ़ने का अभ्यास

For added practice, read about some of the most famous Indian celebrations. Useful vocabulary and cultural notes about the celebrations are given below.

गणतंत्र दिवस २६ जनवरी को मनाते हैं।

होली मार्च में मनाते हैं।

बैसाखी १३ अप्रैल को होती है।

रक्षा बंधन/राखी का त्यौहार अगस्त में होता है।

स्वतंत्रता दिवस १५ अगस्त को मनाते हैं।

विजयदशमी/दशहरा अक्टूबर में होता है।

करवा चौथ अक्टूबर में होता है।

दीपावली/दीवाली अक्टूबर या नवम्बर में होती है।

Vocabulary

गणतंत्र दिवस	Republic Day
मनाना	to celebrate
होली	Holi
बैसाखी	Baisakhi
रक्षा बंधन/राखी	Raksha Bandhan/Rakhi
त्यौहार	festival
स्वतंत्रता दिवस	Independence Day
विजयदशमी/दशहरा	Vijaydashmi/Dusshera
करवा चौथ	Karva Chauth
दीपावली/दीवाली	Deepavali/Diwali

Cultural notes

Some famous Indian celebrations

Republic Day The Indian Republic and the constitution came into effect on January 26, 1950. Also on this day, Hindi was declared the national language of India. Among numerous ceremonies, the Indian prime minister pays homage to the *Amar Jawan Jyoti* (located at the India Gate in New Delhi), soldiers are awarded for their bravery, and a 21-gun salute is given. There is a big parade that takes place in New Delhi.

Holi Because of the Hindu lunar calendar, the date for this festival is variable, but it is generally celebrated in March. On this day, people apply brightly colored paints on each other's faces. This is a very popular festival of colors that welcomes the season of spring.

Baisakhi This festival is celebrated on April 13th. This day marks the New Year for Hindus. Indian farmers celebrate the harvest of their winter crops with singing, dancing, and worship.

Raksha bandhan/Rakhi This occasion is generally celebrated in the month of August. It is meant to strengthen the relationship between a brother and a sister. Sisters tie a decorative thread called *rakhi* on the wrist of their brothers and give them good wishes. In turn, brothers promise to protect their sisters.

Independence Day India gained independence from the British on August 15, 1947. To mark this date, Indians are addressed by the Indian Prime Minister from the Red Fort in New Delhi. The national flag is hoisted and the national anthem is sung.

Vijaydashmi/Dushhera According to the Hindu religious epic *The Ramayan*, the Hindu Lord Shri Ram achieved victory over the Lanka King Ravan on this day. Because Ravan is considered as a symbol of sin, effigies of Ravan and his relatives are burned this day as a symbol of the victory of good over evil. Fairs are held in several places in India and the *Ram Lila* (a show based on the epic) is enacted. Based on the lunar calendar, Vijaydashmi/Dushhera occurs in the month of October.

Karva Chauth On this day, married Indian women keep an all-day fast. The fast begins before sunrise and ends with the viewing of the moon at night. The Hindu Lord Shiv Ji, Mother Parvati (his wife), and Ganesh Ji (his son) are worshipped in the evening. On this day, it is believed that the fast that the women keep will prolong their husbands' lives and increase their prosperity. Karva Chauth is also in the month of October.

Deepavali/Diwali As a follow-up to Vijaydashmi/Dusshera, this day is celebrated as a day of victory of good over evil. According to the Hindu religious epic *The Ramayan*, Shri Ram, his wife Sita, and his brother Laxman returned to their home in Ayodhya after achieving victory over the Lanka King Ravan. People gave him a hearty welcome by decorating their homes with lights. For this reason, Indians celebrate this day by decorating their homes, eating sweets and special dishes, buying new clothes and utensils, worshipping the Hindu goddess Laxmi and Ganesh ji, and setting off a lot of fireworks. Based on the lunar calendar, Deepavali/Diwali occurs in October or November.

Based on the hints given below, name the festival in Hindi.

१. Colors and spring season   _____

२. Fireworks and lights   _____

३. India becomes independent _____

४. Married women fast all day   _____

५. Agricultural harvest   _____

६. India becomes a Republic   _____

७. Brothers and sisters   _____

८. Effigies and fairs   _____

ADJECTIVES
पाठ ६: विशेषण

Grammar

Adjectives
Interrogative word (प्रश्नार्थक शब्द) किस
Interrogative word (प्रश्नार्थक शब्द) कैसा
Comparisons with adjectives
Pronouns in the oblique case
Expressing hunger, thirst, and taste

Vocabulary

Colors
Qualities
Preferences, wants, and needs
Food and drink
Hobbies

Culture

Describing skin tones
Reading practice: Food-related idioms

Describing things
वस्तुओं का वर्णन

Like nouns, adjectives in Hindi are considered either masculine or feminine. The same general principle used for identifying nouns as masculine or feminine applies to adjectives as well—adjectives that end with a consonant or with the diacritic mark for आ are usually masculine, while adjectives that end with the diacritic mark for ई are usually feminine. The rules for converting a masculine or feminine singular to the plural are also the same as for nouns (explained in the previous chapter).

Colors • रंग

The colors listed below have been identified as masculine or feminine and their plural form is also provided, where necessary. As a reminder, masculine adjectives that end with a consonant and feminine adjectives that end with the diacritic mark for ई don't change in their plural version. Therefore, adjectives that end with the diacritic mark for आ are really the ones that have three (*m., f., m. pl.*) different forms.

baby blue	फ़िरोज़ी (*f.*)
black	काला (*m.*), काली (*f.*), काले (*m. pl.*)
blue	नीला (*m.*), नीली (*f.*), नीले (*m. pl.*)
bronze	काँसा (*m.*), काँसे (*m. pl.*)
brown	भूरा (*m.*), भूरी (*f.*), भूरे (*m. pl.*)
golden or blonde	सुनहरा (*m.*), सुनहरी (*f.*), सुनहरे (*m. pl.*)
green	हरा (*m.*), हरी (*f.*), हरे (*m. pl.*)
olive green	मेंहदी (*f.*)
orange	संतरी (*f.*)
pink	गुलाबी (*f.*)
purple or violet	बैंगनी (*f.*)
red	लाल (*m.*)
saffron	भगवा (*m.*)
silver	चाँदी (*f.*)
sky blue	आसमानी (*f.*)
slate gray	स्लेटी (*f.*)
tangerine	नारंगी (*f.*)
white	सफ़ेद (*m.*)
yellow	पीला (*m.*), पीली (*f.*), पीले (*m. pl.*)

Related words used with colors:

pale in color	हल्का (*m.*), हल्की (*f.*), हल्के (*m. pl.*)
	Example: हल्का पीला *light yellow*
dark in color	गहरा (*m.*), गहरी (*f.*), गहरे (*m. pl.*)
	Example: गहरा लाल *dark red*
colorful	रंगीन (*m.*)
multi-colored	रंग-बिरंगा (*m.*), रंग-बिरंगी (*f.*), रंग-बिरंगे (*m. pl.*)

As in English, the placement of adjectives is normally before the noun.

नीली किताब	*blue book*
पीली कुर्सियाँ	*yellow chairs*
हरा बगीचा	*green garden*
भूरे पंखे	*brown fans*
रंग-बिरंगे फूल	*colorful flowers*
रंग-बिरंगी तस्वीरें	*colorful pictures*

Cultural insight

Regarding the color of skin, गोरा (*m.*), गोरी (*f.*), or गोरे (*m. pl.*) is used to refer to people with a light skin tone and/or caucasian background. The word काला (*m.*), काली (*f.*), or काले (*m. pl.*) is used to refer to people with a darker skin tone and/or of African descent. देसी is a slang used by Indians to refer to other Indians.

अभ्यास
१७·१

हिन्दी में लिखिए (*Write in Hindi.*)

१. green plants   _____

२. purple flower   _____

३. brown trees   _____

४. colorful fountain   _____

५. pink bed sheet   _____

६. white pillows   _____

७. red (small) rug   _____

८. golden couch   _____

९. blue doors   _____

१०. orange paintings   _____

Interrogative word (प्रश्नार्थक शब्द) किस

You have already encountered several interrogative words in Hindi: क्या (*what is, what are*) and कहाँ (*where*). Now you will meet a new interrogative word किस, meaning *which*. Used with the postposition का (*of, 's*), it means *of whom* or *whose*. This is the interrogative form used for colors. To ask "*What* color is …?" in Hindi, you would say "*Of which* color is …?"

Of which color is your book?	आपकी किताब किस रंग की है?
My book is blue.	मेरी किताब नीली है।
Of which color is Mira's house?	मीरा का घर किस रंग का है?
Mira's house is yellow.	मीरा का घर पीला है।
Of which color is grass (usually)?	घास किस रंग की होती है?
Grass is (usually) green.	घास हरी होती है।
Whose brown couch is that?	वह भूरा सोफ़ा किस का है?
That brown couch is mine.	वह भूरा सोफ़ा मेरा है।
Whose colorful flowers are those?	वे रंग-बिरंगे फूल किसके हैं?
Those colorful flowers are Kuldeep's.	वे रंग-बिरंगे फूल कुलदीप के हैं।
Whose white books are these?	ये सफ़ेद किताबें किसकी हैं?
These white books are Raveena's.	ये सफ़ेद किताबें रवीना की हैं।

अभ्यास १७·२

हिन्दी में लिखिए (Write in Hindi.)

१. What color is that post office? _____

२. That is slate gray. _____

३. Whose red chairs are these? _____

४. These are Patrick's. _____

५. What color are leaves (usually)? _____

६. They are green (usually). _____

७. What color is that sheet? _____

८. That is green. _____

Qualities • गुणवत्ताएँ

Many adjectives can be used to describe contrasting qualities in nouns, such as *short* vs. *tall*. The adjectives below are in the masculine singular form and need to be modified depending on the number and gender of the noun being described. These opposites have been paired for ease of memorization.

active	चुस्त	*lazy*	सुस्त
beautiful	ख़ूबसूरत/सुन्दर	*ugly*	बदसूरत
brave	साहसी/निडर	*coward*	कायर/डरपोक
clean	साफ़	*dirty*	गंदा
clever	चालाक	*dumb*	मूर्ख
cold	ठंडा	*hot*	गर्म
easy	सरल/आसान	*difficult*	कठिन/मुश्किल
expensive	महँगा	*inexpensive, cheap*	सस्ता
fast	तेज़	*slow*	धीरे
fat, chubby	मोटा	*thin*	पतला
friend	दोस्त/मित्र	*enemy*	दुश्मन/शत्रु
good, nice	अच्छा	*bad*	बुरा
happy	खुश/सुखी	*unhappy*	दुखी
high	ऊँचा	*low*	नीचा
honest	ईमानदार	*dishonest*	बेईमान
lightweight	हल्का	*heavy*	भारी
new	नया	*old (inanimate objects only)*	पुराना
open	खुला	*closed*	बंद
ordinary	आम/साधारण	*special*	ख़ास/विशेष
peaceful, calm	शांत	*chaotic*	अशांत
powerful	ताकतवर	*weak*	कमज़ोर
real	असली	*artificial*	नकली
rich	अमीर/धनी	*poor*	ग़रीब/निर्धन
right	ठीक	*wrong*	ग़लत
short	छोटा	*tall*	लंबा
small	छोटा	*big*	बड़ा
solid	ठोस	*liquid*	तरल
straight	सीधा	*the other way*	उल्टा
		crooked, twisted	टेढ़ा
successful	सफ़ल	*unsuccessful*	असफ़ल
true	सच	*imaginary*	काल्पनिक
wet	गीला	*dry*	सूखा
wide	चौड़ा	*thin*	पतला
young	जवान	*old*	बूढ़ा

कंग फ़ू पैंडा मोटा और बड़ा है।   *Kung Fu Panda is fat and big.*

आपकी कुर्सी छोटी है।   *Your chair is small.*

यह रास्ता सीधा सिनेमाघर जाता है।   *This way goes straight to the movie theater.*

उसका कमरा साफ़ है, पर रीना का कमरा गंदा है।   *His/her room is clean, but Reena's room is dirty.*

वह आदमी मूर्ख नहीं, चालाक है।   *That man is not stupid, (he) is clever.*

क्या यह चीज़ असली है या नकली?   *Is this thing real or artificial?*

अभ्यास १७·३

ठीक या ग़लत? *Mark as true or false.*

१. रुस का मौसम गर्म होता है। _____

२. अमरीकी अभिनेता डैनी डवीटो छोटा है, पर विंस वान लंबा है। _____

३. पानी एक गीली ठोस चीज़ है। _____

४. ताज महल एक ख़ूबसूरत इमारत है। _____

५. झुम्पा लहरी एक सफ़ल वकील है। _____

अभ्यास १७·४

Circle the adjective that fits the sentence.

१. यह लड़की छोटा, छोटी, छोटे है।

२. वह मोटा, मोटी, मोटे आदमी है।

३. ये कलाकार अच्छा, अच्छे, अच्छी हैं।

४. फूलदान में फूल ख़ूबसूरत, ख़ूबसूरते हैं।

५. घर में सीढ़ियाँ चौड़ा, चौड़ी, चौड़े हैं।

६. वे लोग गर्म, गर्मे मौसम में रहते हैं।

७. वे लड़के लंबा, लंबी, लंबे हैं।

८. ये तकिए हल्का, हल्की, हल्के हैं।

९. दरवाज़े खुला, खुली, खुले हैं।

१०. लोग खुश, खुशे हैं।

११. यह कंबल मँहगा, महँगी, महँगे है, सस्ता नहीं।

१२. दीवार पर ख़ास, ख़ासे तस्वीरें हैं।

१३. वे औरतें अमीर, अमीरी और सफ़ल हैं।

१४. भारत में महँगी चीज़ें आम, आमी बात है।

१५. वह इमारत पुराना, पुरानी, पुराने और शांत है।

Comparisons
तुलनाएँ

Interrogative word (प्रश्नार्थक शब्द) कैसा

The interrogative word कैसा means *how*. It changes with the gender and number of the noun that is being inquired about; consequently, कैसा has three forms:

कैसा (*m.*), कैसी (*f.*), and कैसे (*m. pl.*)

Here is how it is used:

मद्रास में आज मौसम कैसा है?	*How is the weather in Madras today?*
गर्म है।	*(It) is hot.*
आपकी माता जी कैसी हैं?	*How is your mom?*
वे ठीक हैं।	*She is alright.*
आप कैसे हैं?	*How are you?*
मैं अच्छा हूँ।	*I am well.*

Note: As an adverb, कैसे also means *how*, but it does not change. This form is used to find out how something is done or about the procedure of something. For example:

(आप) गाड़ी कैसे चलाते हैं?	*How do (you) drive a car?*

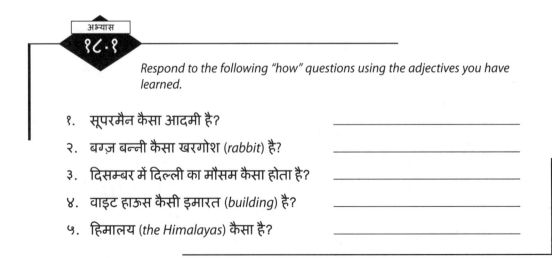

अभ्यास
१८·१

Respond to the following "how" questions using the adjectives you have learned.

१. सूपरमैन कैसा आदमी है? _____

२. बग्ज़ बन्नी कैसा खरगोश (*rabbit*) है? _____

३. दिसम्बर में दिल्ली का मौसम कैसा होता है? _____

४. वाइट हाऊस कैसी इमारत (*building*) है? _____

५. हिमालय (*the Himalayas*) कैसा है? _____

Provide the "how" questions that will receive the answers provided.

१. _____

जून में अमरीका का मौसम गर्म होता है।

२. _____

मेरा बगीचा हरा और ख़ूबसूरत है। (*Use formal* your)

३. _____

यह प्रश्न (*question*) आसान है।

४. _____

मेरा कुत्ता (*dog*) साहसी, ताकतवर, और तेज़ है। (*Use formal* your)

५. _____

यह बात नई है।

Comparisons using adjectives • विशेषण के साथ तुलना

Adjectives can be further used to make comparisons between nouns. In Hindi, it is common to use the postposition से as *than* when making a comparison:

than	से
less than	से कम
little … than	से थोड़ा, थोड़ी, थोड़े
more than	से ज़्यादा
very, a lot	बहुत
quite, enough	काफ़ी
the most	सबसे
better than	से बेहतर, अच्छा

Note: You can say that something is "worse than" by using से कम या से ज़्यादा with the quality that is being highlighted.

सुनील रमन से चालाक है।	*Sunil is cleverer than Raman.*
सुनील रमन से ज़्यादा ईमानदार है।	*Sunil is more honest than Raman.*
वह आम आदमी से कम ताकतवर है।	*He is less powerful than an ordinary man.*
राम श्याम से थोड़ा पतला है।	*Ram is a little slimmer than Shyam.*
क्या वह सबसे तेज़ है?	*Is s/he the fastest?*
मेरा कमरा सबसे साफ़ है।	*My room is the cleanest.*
यह बेहतर है।	*This is better.*
उनका घर काफ़ी अच्छा है।	*Their house is quite nice.*

Supply the correct comparative to complete the following sentences.

१. Is he the richest?

क्या वह _____ अमीर है?

२. You (*formal*) are taller than Mohini.

आप मोहिनी _____ लंबे हैं।

३. Dinesh is less fat than Ramesh.

दिनेश रमेश _____ मोटा है।

४. Nargis is more beautiful than Anjana.

नरगिस अंजना _____ ख़ूबसूरत है।

५. The son sleeps the most.

बेटा _____ सोता है।

Pronouns in the oblique case (with all postpositions) • सर्वनाम के कारक-रूप

You have seen most of the basic postpositions in Hindi—में, पर, को, से, का, की, के—and you will encounter compound postpositions in the next chapter. It is important to know that whenever any postposition is directly used with a pronoun, the oblique case of the pronoun must be used (just as in English, one uses *give him*, not *give he*).

Here is the oblique case of each of the pronouns:

मैं	*becomes*	मुझ
तू	*becomes*	तुझ
तुम	*remains*	तुम
आप	*remains*	आप
हम	*remains*	हम
यह	*becomes*	इस
वह	*becomes*	उस
ये	*becomes*	इन
वे	*becomes*	उन

Notice the placement of the oblique pronoun in the following examples. The first pronoun is *not* in the oblique case because the postposition is not used with that pronoun, while the second pronoun turns into oblique because of the postposition.

वह मुझ से लंबा है।	*He is taller than me.*
तुम उस से ज़्यादा ईमानदार हो।	*You are more honest than him/her.*
फूल इस फूलदान में डालते हैं।	*Flowers are put in this vase.*
क्या वे लोग इन से ज़्यादा अच्छे हैं?	*Are those people better than these?*
यह औरत उस औरत से कम चुस्त है।	*This woman is less active than that woman.*

Underline the oblique pronouns in these sentences and place an X next to the sentence if it is used incorrectly.

१. यह टी.वी. उस टी.वी. से ज़्यादा महँगा है।   _____

२. उस घर से यह घर बेहतर है।   _____

३. मुझ से माता जी प्रश्न पूछते हैं।   _____

४. तुम वह से डरता है।   _____

५. मेरा लैपटाप उन के लैपटाप से कम भारी है।   _____

हिन्दी में लिखिए *(Translate.)*

१. This museum is bigger than that museum.   _____

२. We keep the fan on this table.   _____

३. You (*formal*) talk (बात करना) with them.   _____

४. They talk with you (*informal*).   _____

५. You (*informal*) shake hands with me.   _____

Preferences, wants, and needs • पसंद, इच्छाएँ, व आवश्यकताएँ

Special note about को:

A short oblique form also exists with the postposition को:

मुझको	=	मुझे
तुझको	=	तुझे
आपको	=	आपको
हमको	=	हमें
इसको	=	इसे
उसको	=	उसे
इनको	=	इन्हें
उनको	=	उन्हें

Preferences, wants, or needs are typically expressed using certain verbs with को:

को पसंद होना	*to like, prefer, find pleasing*
को अच्छा लगना	*to like, find pleasing*
को चाहना	*to like (with a noun), to want to (with a verb)*
को चाहिए	*to need (with a noun), to ought to/should (with a verb)*

Like or dislike can be expressed for a person, place, or thing (noun), or an action (verb). When expressing like or dislike regarding an action, the entire verb is used in the infinitive. For example, I like *to watch* TV would be मुझे टी.वी. देखना पसंद है। Also, while other three verbs are conjugated like regular Hindi verbs, चाहिए is an imperative form and doesn't change with the noun or verb of preference.

Here are more examples illustrating how to express like or dislike:

क्या आपको दिल्ली पसंद है?	*Do you like Delhi?*
राकेश को यह लड़की पसंद नहीं।	*Rakesh does not like this girl.*
तुझे बाग में सैर करना पसंद है।	*You like to stroll in the garden.*
उसे हमारा काम अच्छा लगता है।	*S/He likes our work.*
इस लड़की को राकेश अच्छा नहीं लगता।	*This girl does not like Rakesh.*
तुम्हें गाड़ी चलाना अच्छा लगता है?	*Do you like to drive (a car)?*
मैं गौरव को चाहती हूँ।	*I like Gaurav.*
वह समोसा खाना चाहता है।	*He wants to eat a samosa.*
मैं बाज़ार जाना नहीं चाहती।	*I don't want to go to the market.*
मुझे नई गाड़ी चाहिए।	*I need a new car.*
इसे घर आना चाहिए।	*S/He should come home.*
इन्हें रविवार को काम नहीं करना चाहिए।	*They should not work on a Sunday.*

अभ्यास
१८·६

अनुवाद कीजिए *(Translate.)*

१. I like to read books. _____

२. I don't like to get up in the morning. _____

३. At night, she ought to sleep. _____

४. They need a new house. _____

५. He likes Susan. _____

६. Reema doesn't like to work on a Monday. _____

Food and drink
भोजन व पेय

Food and drink • भोजन व पेय

Cultural insight

As you might have heard, seen, or even tasted, Indian food is quite different from other Western-style cuisines and a significant part of the whole Indian cultural experience. The diet consists of handmade breads or rice with prepared vegetables, beans, or meats. Sides or accompaniments to the meal include chutneys, salads, yogurt, and pickles. There are several dessert and beverage options.

♦ Main grains (अनाज) and their flours (आटा) include:

barley flour	जौं (*f.*) का आटा
chick peas/garbanzo beans (gram) flour	बेसन (*m.*)
corn flour	मक्की (*f.*) का आटा
rice	चावल (*m.*)
semolina flour	सूजी (*f.*)
white flour	मैदा (*m.*)
whole wheat flour	गेहूँ (*f.*) का आटा (*m.*)

♦ These flours are used to prepare handmade breads such as:

fried wheat bread	पूरी (*f.*)
fried sourdough flatbread	भट्टूरे (*m. pl.*)
layered wheat flatbread with vegetable stuffing	पराँठा (*m.*)
oven-baked wheat flatbread	तंदूरी रोटी (*f.*)
oven-baked yeast flatbread	नान (*m.*)
tubular rice crepe	डोसा (*m.*)
wheat flatbread	रोटी (*f.*), चपाती (*f.*)

- Main vegetables (सब्ज़ियाँ) and beans (दालें) are:

bell pepper	शिमला मिर्च (*f.*)
bitter gourd	करेला (*m.*)
black or white chick peas/garbanzo beans	काले या सफ़ेद चने (*m.*), छोले (*m.*)
black-eyed peas	लोबिया (*m.*)
cabbage	पत्तागोभी (*f.*), बंदगोभी (*f.*)
carrot	गाजर (*f.*)
cauliflower	फूलगोभी (*f.*)
curry	कड़ी (*f.*)
daikon radish	मूली (*f.*)
dal/lentil	दाल (*f.*)
eggplant	बैंगन (*m.*)
jackfruit	कटहल (*m.*)
mushroom	मशरूम (*m.*)
okra	भिंडी (*f.*)
peas	मटर (*m.*)
potato	आलू (*m.*)
pumpkin	कद्दू (*m.*)
red kidney beans	राजमा (*m.*)
spinach	पालक (*f.*)
string beans	फ़लियाँ (*f.*)
sweet potato	शकरकंद (*f.*)
turnip	शलगम (*m.*)

- Some of the prepared dishes include:

buttered black lentils	दाल मक्खनी
buttered chicken in a tomato and yogurt gravy	मुर्ग मक्खनी
mashed eggplant	बैंगन भरता
mixed vegetables	नवरत्न कोरमा
mutton curry	रोगन जोश
mutton in yogurt gravy	शाही कोरमा
peas and cheese	मटर पनीर
peas and mushroom	मटर मशरूम
potato and cauliflower	आलू गोभी
potato and peas	आलू मटर
rice and lentils cooked together	खिचड़ी
rice with mixed vegetables	पुलाव/बिरयानी

roasted chicken	मुर्ग़ मुसल्लम
roasted marinated fish	मच्छी टिक्का
shish kabob	बोटी कबाब
spicy chick peas/garbanzo beans	चना मसाला
spicy curried prawns	मसालेदार झींगा
spicy skewered meat	सीख कबाब
spinach with cheese	पालक/साग पनीर

◆ The following are used for salads, chutneys, and condiments:

cucumber	खीरा (m.)
garlic	लहसुन (m.)
ginger	अदरक (m.)
green chili peppers	हरी मिर्च (f.)
lemon	नींबू (m.)
mint	पुदीना (m.)
onion	प्याज़ (m.)
parsley	हरा धनिया (m.)
tamarind	इमली (f.)
tomato	टमाटर (m.)

◆ Non vegetarian and seafood includes:

chicken	मुर्ग़ (m.)
crab	केंकड़ा (m.)
fish	मछली (f.)
minced meat	कीमा (m.)
prawn or shrimp	झींगा (m.)
sheep or lamb meat	मटन (m.)

◆ Dairy items:

butter	मक्खन (m.)
buttermilk	छाछ (f.)
clarified butter	घी (m.)
egg	अंडा (m.)
farmer's cheese	पनीर (m.)
homemade ice cream	कुल्फ़ी (f.)
ice-cream with noodles	फ़लूदा (m.)
milk	दूध (m.)
yogurt shake	लस्सी (f.)
yogurt with cucumber and herbs	रायता (m.)
yogurt	दही (m.)

- Main fruits are:

apple	सेब (*m.*)
banana	केला (*m.*)
coconut	नारियल (*m.*)
dates	खजूर (*f.*)
fig	अंजीर (*f.*)
grapes	अंगूर (*m.*)
guava	अमरूद (*m.*)
kiwi look-alike fruit	चीकू (*m.*)
litchi	लीची (*f.*)
mango	आम (*m.*)
melon	खरबूजा (*m.*)
orange	संतरा (*m.*)
papaya	पपीता (*m.*)
peach	आड़ू (*m.*)
pear	नाशपति (*f.*)
pineapple	अनानास (*m.*)
purple berry	जामुन (*m.*)
watermelon	तरबूज (*m.*)

- Nuts, spices, condiments, and oils:

all-purpose hot spice	गर्म मसाला (*m.*)
almonds	बादाम (*m.*)
bay leaves	तेज़पत्र (*m.*)
black pepper	काली मिर्च (*f.*)
cane sugar	गुड़ (*m.*)
cardamom	इलायची (*f.*)
cashews	काजू (*m.*)
cinnamon	दालचीनी (*f.*)
cloves	लौंग (*m.*)
cumin seed	जीरा (*m.*)
fennel seed	सौंफ़ (*f.*)
honey	शहद (*m.*)
mustard oil	सरसों का तेल (*m.*)
mustard	राई (*f.*)
olive oil	जैतून का तेल (*m.*)
peanuts	मूँगफ़लियाँ (*f. pl.*)
pickle	अचार (*m.*)

pistachios	पिस्ता (m.)
raisins	किशमिश (f.)
red chili pepper	लाल मिर्च (f.)
salt	नमक (m.)
sesame seed	तिल (m.)
sugar	चीनी (f.)
turmeric	हल्दी (f.)
vinegar	सिरका (m.)
walnuts	अखरोट (m.)
yeast	खमीर (f.)

- ◆ Some savory snacks:

pastry puff filled with tamarind water	गोलगप्पे
potato patties	टिक्कियाँ (f. pl.)
savory mixture	चाट (f.)
spicy wafer	पापड़ (m.)
vegetable fritters	पकोड़े (m. pl.)
vegetable puff pastry	समोसे (m. pl.)

- ◆ Main sweets

carrot pudding	गाजर का हलवा (m.)
cheese patties in thickened milk	रसमलाई (f.)
cold cheese dumpling in sweet syrup	रसगुल्ला (m.)
hot cheese dumpling in sweet syrup	गुलाब जामुन (m.)
rice pudding	खीर (f.)
semolina flour pudding	हलवा (m.)
small cheese cakes	बर्फ़ी (f.)
sweet pretzel filled with syrup	जलेबी (f.)

- ◆ Main beverages:

alcohol (wine, beer, and spirits)	शराब (f.)
chai (masala chai)	मसाला चाय (f.)
coffee	काफ़ी (f.)
juice	रस (m.)
lemonade	शिकंजवीं (f.)
soft drink	कोल्ड ड्रिंक (m.)
water	पानी (m.)
yogurt shake	लस्सी (f.)

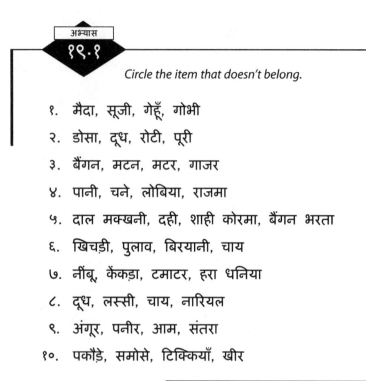

Circle the item that doesn't belong.

१. मैदा, सूजी, गेहूँ, गोभी

२. डोसा, दूध, रोटी, पूरी

३. बैंगन, मटन, मटर, गाजर

४. पानी, चने, लोबिया, राजमा

५. दाल मक्खनी, दही, शाही कोरमा, बैंगन भरता

६. खिचड़ी, पुलाव, बिरयानी, चाय

७. नींबू, केंकड़ा, टमाटर, हरा धनिया

८. दूध, लस्सी, चाय, नारियल

९. अंगूर, पनीर, आम, संतरा

१०. पकौड़े, समोसे, टिक्कियाँ, खीर

Read the following paragraph explaining what Indians typically eat for breakfast, lunch, and dinner. (Do not worry about words or constructions that you have not seen so far. A translation is provided below. Just pick out as much detail as you can.)

आम तौर पर, भारतीय लोग नाश्ते में परांठे के साथ मक्खन या घी और गर्म चाय या दूध लेते हैं। दोपहर के खाने में सब्ज़ी के साथ रोटी, नान, पूरी, या भटूरे लेते हैं। कई लोग साथ में रायता, लस्सी, या सलाद भी पसंद करते हैं। रात के खाने में वे दाल और सब्ज़ी के साथ रोटी, चावल आदि खाना पसंद करते हैं।

Translation

Usually, Indian people take paranthas with butter or ghee and hot tea or milk for breakfast. At lunch, they take roti, nan, puri, or bhature with vegetable. Some people like raita, lassi, or salad with it. For dinner, they like dal and vegetable with roti, rice, etc.

List five new Indian food items in the passage above that you might like to try.

१. _____

२. _____

३. _____

४. _____

५. _____

Hunger, thirst, and taste • भूख, प्यास, व स्वाद

The verb लगना is used mostly with experiences (such as hunger, thirst, cold, heat, etc.) and it takes the postposition को.

to be hungry	को भूख लगना
to be thirsty	को प्यास लगना

मुझे भूख लगी है।	*I am hungry.*
मुझे प्यास लगी है।	*I am thirsty.*

को लगना is also used to express different tastes that are experienced with foods and drinks:

मुझे दही <u>खट्टा</u> लगता है।	*I find yogurt to be sour/tangy.*
मुझे करेला <u>कड़वा</u> लगता है।	*I find bitter gourd to be bitter.*
मुझे केला <u>मीठा</u> लगता है।	*I find banana to be sweet.*
मुझे आम पापड़ <u>खट्टा-मीठा</u> लगता है।	*I find mango wafer to be sweet and sour.*
मुझे समोसा <u>नमकीन</u> लगता है।	*I find puff pastry to be salty/savory.*
मुझे फ़ल <u>ताज़ा</u> लगता है।	*I find fruit to be fresh.*
मुझे परसों का मक्खन <u>बासी</u> लगता है।	*I find day before yesterday's butter to be stale.*
मुझे रसगुल्ला <u>नर्म</u> लगता है।	*I find cold cheese dumpling to be soft.*
मुझे कटहल <u>सख़्त</u> लगता है।	*I find jackfruit to be hard.*
मुझे चना मसाला <u>मसालेदार</u> लगता है।	*I find spiced chick peas to be spicy.*
मुझे पानी <u>फ़ीका</u> लगता है।	*I find water to be bland.*

Note: As नमकीन, बासी, नर्म, सख़्त, and मसालेदार end with a consonant, they remain unchanged. However, as खट्टा, कड़वा, मीठा, खट्टा-मीठा, ताज़ा, and फ़ीका end with आ, they change based on the number and gender of the noun they modify.

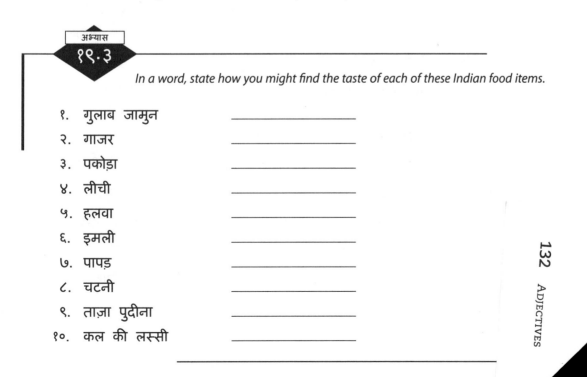

अभ्यास
१९·३

In a word, state how you might find the taste of each of these Indian food items.

१. गुलाब जामुन   _____

२. गाजर   _____

३. पकोड़ा   _____

४. लीची   _____

५. हलवा   _____

६. इमली   _____

७. पापड़   _____

८. चटनी   _____

९. ताज़ा पुदीना   _____

१०. कल की लस्सी   _____

Hobbies • शौक/रुचियाँ

What do you like to do in your free time?

ख़ाली समय में आप क्या करना पसंद करते हैं?

What are you hobbies?

आपके क्या शौक हैं?

to box	मुक्केबाज़ी करना	to play video games	विडियो खेल खेलना
to camp	शिविर लगाना	to read a magazine	पत्रिका पढ़ना
to canoe	नौका विहार करना	to ride a bicycle	साईकल चलाना
to dive	गोताखोरी करना	to ride a horse	घुड़सवारी करना
to embroider	कढ़ाई करना	to roam on the beach	समुद्र तट पर घूमना
to exercise	व्यायाम, कसरत करना	to rock climb	पर्वतारोहण करना
to fence	तलवारबाज़ी करना	to roller skate	रोलरस्केटिंग करना
to fish	मछली पकड़ना	to row	नाव खेना
to garden	बागबानी करना	to sail, raft	नौकायन करना
to go for a drive	गाड़ी में घूमना	to ski	स्कीइंग करना
to go to a concert	कांसर्ट जाना	to skydive	आकाशीय गोताखोरी करना
to hike	पदयात्रा करना	to snow board	स्नोबोर्डिंग करना
to knit	बुनना	to solve puzzles	पहेलियाँ बूझना
to paint or draw	चित्रकारी करना	to spend time with family	परिवार के साथ समय बिताना
to play baseball	बेसबाल खेलना	to stroll in the park	पार्क में सैर करना
to play basketball	बास्केटबाल खेलना	to surf (wind, water)	सर्फ़िंग करना
to play chess	शतरंज खेलना	to swim	तैरना
to play hockey	हाकी खेलना	to take photos	फोटो खींचना
to play golf	गोल्फ़ खेलना	to watch movies	फ़िल्में देखना
to play soccer	साकर खेलना	to watch TV	टी.वी. देखना
to play volleyball	वालीबाल खेलना	to wrestle	कुश्ती करना
to play cricket	क्रिकेट खेलना	to write stories	कहानियाँ लिखना
to play racquetball	रैकेटबाल खेलना		

Match the noun with the appropriate hobby verb.

१.	पानी		फ़ोटो खींचना
२.	टी.वी.		मुक्केबाज़ी
३.	गाड़ी		साईकल चलाना
४.	बास्केट		बागबानी करना
५.	दो लोग		मछली पकड़ना
६.	मुक्का		टी.वी. देखना
७.	साईकल		गाड़ी में घूमना
८.	बाग		बास्केटबाल खेलना
९.	कैमरा		तैरना, गोताखोरी
१०.	मछली		कुश्ती करना

Put an X next to the statement that is likely to be false.

१. माईकल फ़ैल्प्सः मुझे तैरना पसंद है। _____

२. डरपोक आदमीः मैं आकाशीय गोताखोरी करना चाहता हूँ। _____

३. लैंस आर्मस्ट्रोंगः मुझे साईकल चलाना अच्छा लगता है। _____

४. मारथा स्टूअर्टः मुझे मुक्केबाज़ी अच्छी लगती है। _____

५. मुहम्मद अलीः मैं कढ़ाई करना चाहता हूँ। _____

६. दले लामाः मुझे तलवारबाज़ी करनी चाहिए। _____

७. लेखकः मुझे कुश्ती करना पसंद है। _____

८. सर्फ़रः मैं पानी से डरता हूँ। _____

९. बच्चाः मुझे विडियो खेल खेलना पसंद है। _____

१०. माईकल जोर्डनः मुझे बास्केटबाल खेलना पसंद है। _____

Use these verbs that you encountered in the last section and talk about some of your hobbies or activities that you like to do. What are some activities that you don't like to do? Discuss activities that you might like to try.

को पसंद होना	*to like, prefer, find pleasing*
को अच्छा लगना	*to like, find pleasing*
को चाहना	*to like* (with a noun), *to want to* (with a verb)
को चाहिए	*to need* (with a noun), *to ought to/should* (with a verb)

_____

_____

_____

_____

_____

_____

Reading practice • पढ़ने का अभ्यास

Food is incorporated into some very colorful Hindi idioms. Read the following expressions. A literal meaning is also provided.

1. मक्खन लगाना: *To sweet talk*
   (Literally: *to apply butter*)

2. टेढ़ी खीर होना: *For an endeavor to be difficult*
   (Literally: *to be a crooked rice pudding*)

3. अपनी खिचड़ी अलग पकाना: *To do one's own thing separately*
   (Literally: *to cook one's own rice and lentil mixture separately*)

4. जले पर नमक छिड़कना: *To add fuel to fire*
   (Literally: *to sprinkle salt on a burn*)

5. दूध का दूध, पानी का पानी करना: *To isolate the truth from the untruth and achieve justice*
   (Literally: *to isolate milk and water from mixed milk and water*)

6. घर की मुर्गी दाल बराबर समझना: *To take an expensive asset for granted because it is easily accessible*
   (Literally: *to equate the domesticated chicken, normally more expensive outside, to cheaper lentils*)

   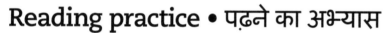

7. कीमा बनाना: *To beat someone up*
   (Literally: *to mince meat*)

8. दाल में कुछ काला होना: *To smell a rat*
   (Literally: *for something black to be found in dal*)

9. पानी पानी होना: *To be embarrassed*
   (Literally: *to be liquidated into water*)

10. घी के दिए जलाना: *To celebrate with joy*
    (Literally: *to light earthen lamps with ghee*)

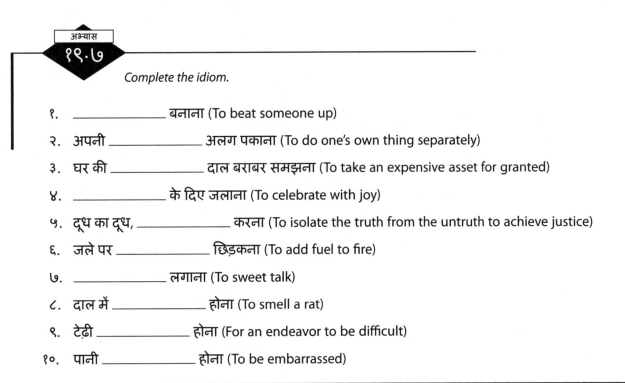

अभ्यास
१९·७

Complete the idiom.

१. _____ बनाना (To beat someone up)

२. अपनी _____ अलग पकाना (To do one's own thing separately)

३. घर की _____ दाल बराबर समझना (To take an expensive asset for granted)

४. _____ के दिए जलाना (To celebrate with joy)

५. दूध का दूध, _____ करना (To isolate the truth from the untruth to achieve justice)

६. जले पर _____ छिड़कना (To add fuel to fire)

७. _____ लगाना (To sweet talk)

८. दाल में _____ होना (To smell a rat)

९. टेढ़ी _____ होना (For an endeavor to be difficult)

१०. पानी _____ होना (To be embarrassed)

POSTPOSITIONS AND THE PAST TENSE

पाठ ७: कारक व भूतकाल

Grammar

Adjectives in the oblique case
Nouns in the oblique case
Possessives in the oblique case
Ways to say *to have*
Interrogative word (प्रश्नार्थक शब्द) कितना
Postposition को
The imperative
The past tense

Vocabulary

Wild and domestic animals
Parts of the body
The senses
Body ailments
Compound postpositions
Some more useful verbs
Travel and directions
Reading practice: Vocabulary

Culture

Reading practice: Recipe for Masala Chai

Postpositions
कारक

Postpositions: Adjectives in the oblique case • विशेषण के कारक-रूप

Like pronouns, adjectives (colors, qualities, tastes, etc.) used with postpositions must also be in their oblique case. This affects mainly the adjectives that end in the diacritic mark for आ, such as पीला, अच्छा, मीठा, and so on. Other adjectives that end in a consonant or the diacritic mark for ई, such as साफ़ या साहसी, do not change. To make things simpler, the oblique form for adjectives that end in -आ looks exactly like their plural form.

For example, अच्छा बच्चा, when used with any postposition, say को, becomes:

<u>अच्छे</u> बच्चे को	*to the* <u>good</u> *child* (singular)
<u>अच्छे</u> बच्चों को	*to the* <u>good</u> *children* (plural)

Note: You may have noticed that the noun बच्चा also changes into the oblique. This is explained in more detail in the nouns section below. For now, let's focus on adjectives.

Adjectives that end with a consonant or the diacritic mark for ई do not change in the oblique case. साफ़ बच्चा when used with the postposition को becomes:

<u>साफ़</u> बच्चे को	*to the* <u>clean</u> *child* (singular)
<u>साफ़</u> बच्चों को	*to the* <u>clean</u> *children* (plural)

Similarly, साहसी बच्चा when used with a postposition को becomes:

<u>साहसी</u> बच्चे को	*to the* <u>brave</u> *child* (singular)
<u>साहसी</u> बच्चों को	*to the* <u>brave</u> *child* (plural)

Write the following adjectives in the oblique case.

१. in the *small* house   _____ घर में

२. in the *small* houses   _____ घरों में

3. on the *big* rug   _____ दरी पर

४. on the *big* rugs   _____ दरियों पर

५. to the *beautiful* woman   _____ औरत को

६. to the *beautiful* women   _____ औरतों को

७. from the *thin* man   _____ आदमी से

८. from the *thin* men   _____ आदमियों से

९. of the *high* mountain   _____ पहाड़ का

१०. of the *high* mountains   _____ पहाड़ों का

११. up to the *yellow* chair   _____ कुर्सी तक

१२. up to the *yellow* chairs   _____ कुर्सियों तक

Add the oblique case of pronouns along with the oblique case of adjectives.

१. in *that small* house   _____ घर में

२. in *those small* houses   _____ घरों में

3. on *her big* rug   _____ दरी पर

४. on *her big* rugs   _____ दरियों पर

५. to *that beautiful* woman   _____ औरत को

६. to *those beautiful* women   _____ औरतों को

७. from *this thin* man   _____ आदमी से

८. from *these thin* men   _____ आदमियों से

९. of *that high* mountain   _____ पहाड़ का

१०. of *those high* mountains   _____ पहाड़ों का

११. up to *his yellow* chair   _____ कुर्सी तक

१२. up to *his yellow* chairs   _____ कुर्सियों तक

Postpositions: Nouns in the oblique case • संज्ञा के कारक-रूप

Along with pronouns and adjectives, nouns used with postpositions must also be in their oblique case. Here is a breakdown of how masculine and feminine nouns change to their oblique cases.

Masculine oblique cases

1. Masculine nouns that end with a consonant, such as अध्यापक or चिड़ियाघर, stay the same in the singular oblique, but change with an -ओं ending in the plural oblique.

to the teacher	अध्यापक को	*to the teachers*	अध्यापकों को
to the zoo	चिड़ियाघर को	*to the zoos*	चिड़ियाघरों को

2. Masculine nouns that end with the diacritic mark for आ, such as बेटा or बगीचा, change into the singular oblique by adding the diacritic mark for ए and into the plural oblique with the -ओं ending.

to the son	बेटे को	*to the sons*	बेटों को
to the garden	बगीचे को	*to the gardens*	बगीचों को

3. Certain masculine singular nouns that end with the diacritic mark for आ, such as पिता or विक्रेता, stay the same in the singular oblique, but change in the plural oblique with an -ओं ending.

to the father	पिता को	*to the fathers*	पिताओं को
to the seller	विक्रेता को	*to the sellers*	विक्रेताओं को

4. Masculine singular nouns that end with other vowels (aside from आ), such as आलू or नींबू, stay the same in the singular oblique, but change in the plural by shortening the previous vowel and adding the -ओं ending.

to the potato	आलू को	*to the potatoes*	आलुओं को
to the lemon	नींबू को	*to the lemons*	नींबुओं को

Feminine oblique cases

Most feminine singular nouns stay the same in the singular oblique, but change in the plural with an ओं ending. You just have to remember how to add the ओं to the various feminine noun endings:

to the book	किताब को	*to the books*	किताबों को
to the mother	माता को	*to the mothers*	माताओं को
to the sparrow	चिड़िया को	*to the sparrows*	चिड़ियों को
to the daughter-in-law	बहू को	*to the daughter-in-laws*	बहुओं को
to the actress	अभिनेत्री को	*to the actresses*	अभिनेत्रियों को

Translate using the oblique form of nouns.

१. from the son; from the sons _____

२. in the airport; in the airports _____

३. of the father; of the fathers _____

४. on the pumpkin; on the pumpkins _____

५. from the daughter; from the daughters _____

६. to the mom; to the moms _____

७. of the sister; of the sisters _____

८. on the doll; on the dolls _____

Translate by using the oblique cases of pronouns, adjectives, and nouns together.

१. from that good son; from those good sons

_____

२. in this big airport; in these big airports

_____

३. of this old father; of these old fathers

_____

४. on this golden pumpkin; on these golden pumpkins

_____

५. from that beautiful daughter; from those beautiful daughters

_____

६. to my good mom; to my good moms

_____

७. of his younger sister; of his younger sisters

_____

८. on her expensive doll; on her expensive dolls

_____

Write full sentences in Hindi.

१. These brown cabinets are in my old kitchen.

_____

२. This beautiful flower is in this expensive vase.

_____

३. Are those bananas from that small garden?

_____

४. These beautiful curtains are on those wide windows.

_____

५. The colorful pictures are on those French doors.

_____

अभ्यास

२०.६

ठीक या ग़लत? *Mark whether the oblique cases used are correct or incorrect.*

१. हम इस गंदे फ़र्श पर झाड़ू लगाते हैं।   _____

२. उस नर्म सोफ़ा पर बच्चे बैठते हैं।   _____

३. वे नाश्ते में ताज़े अंडे खाते हैं।   _____

४. तुम इस गर्म परांठे पर ठंडा मक्खन रखते हो?   _____

५. मैं को बहुत प्यास लगी है।   _____

६. उस खुले दरवाज़े की चाबी नहीं है।   _____

७. लोग उन से लंबी बातें करते हैं।   _____

८. इस मीठी खीर में काफ़ी चीनी है।   _____

९. हमारी हरी चादरों पर खूबसूरत तस्वीरें हैं।   _____

१०. लोग ताज़े खीरा पर काली मिर्च और नींबू लगाना पसंद करते हैं।   _____

Postpositions: Possessives in the oblique case • संबंधकारक के कारक-रुप

The possessive oblique case is fairly simple. When a postposition is used, all masculine singular possessives are changed into their oblique form—the masculine plural possessive. The feminine possessives remain unchanged.

मेरा घर	मेरे घर में	*in my house*
तेरा परिवार	तेरे परिवार में	*in your family*
तुम्हारा छोटा भाई	तुम्हारे छोटे भाई को	*to your younger brother*
आपका सेब	आपके सेब का	*of your apple*
हमारा ताज़ा दही	हमारे ताज़े दही से	*from our fresh yogurt*
इसका पुराना दफ़्तर	इसके पुराने दफ़्तर से	*from his/her old office*
उसका पानी का गिलास	उसके पानी के गिलास में	*in his/her glass of water*
इनका सफ़ेद काग़ज़	इनके सफ़ेद काग़ज़ पर	*on their white paper*
उनका हरा पेड़	उनके हरे पेड़ पर	*on their green tree*

The same is also applicable to का used separately with a noun.

रमा का छोटा भाई	रमा के छोटे भाई को	*to Rama's younger brother*
दिल्ली की एक इमारत	दिल्ली की एक इमारत में	*in a building in Delhi*

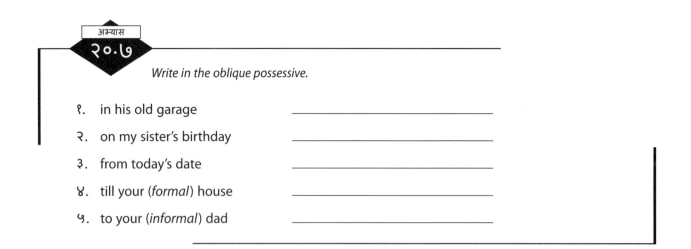

अभ्यास
२०·७

Write in the oblique possessive.

१. in his old garage   _____

२. on my sister's birthday   _____

३. from today's date   _____

४. till your (*formal*) house   _____

५. to your (*informal*) dad   _____

Ways of saying *to have*

As a specific verb, *to have* does not exist in Hindi. However, there are a variety of ways to indicate possession. You have already seen the use of the possessives and the postpositions का, की, के (*of*, *'s*). These are used particularly for things having to do with the body, such as clothes; emotions; kinship terms; and stationary assets such as land, house, garden, and so on.

पूनम की टोपी	*Poonam's hat*
रुतिका का गुस्सा	*Rutika's anger*
नीना के भाई	*Nina's brothers*
मेरे पिता जी की ज़मीन	*My father's land*

Movable assets such as animals, vehicles, time, and money require the use of the compound postposition के पास, which roughly translates as "near to," but carries the sense of ownership. Another way to say *to have* is with the postposition को that is used with bodily ailments. This is explained later in the chapter.

Some useful words to know

something, some (a bunch of)	कुछ
nothing	कुछ नहीं
someone, some (a particular noun)	कोई
no one, nobody	कोई नहीं
several	कई
time	समय, वक़्त (*m.*)
money	पैसा (*m.*)

मेरे पास तीन गाड़ियाँ हैं।	*I have three cars.*
सुमित के पास समय नहीं है।	*Sumit does not have time.*
उसके पास कितना पैसा है?	*How much money does he/she have?*

Interrogative word (प्रश्नार्थक शब्द) कितना

The interrogative word कितना means *how much/many* and changes with the number and gender of the noun: कितना (*m.*), कितनी (*f.*), and कितने (*m. pl.*). To ask "How much is something" in Hindi is to ask "Of how much is something," meaning that postpositions का, की, के are used in conjunction with the correct form of कितना. (**Note:** The Indian currency is called the *rupee*: रुपया (*m.*). The plural form is रुपए/रुपये and the abbreviated form is रु.) कितना can also be used to make a statement. For example:

आप के कितने घर हैं?	*How many houses do you have?*
रुपा के पास कितनी किताबें हैं?	*How many books does Rupa have?*
ये केले कितने के हैं?	*How much are these bananas?*
ये ४० रुपये के हैं।	*They are 40 rupees.*
यह ख़रबूजा कितने का है?	*How much is this melon?*
यह ५० रुपये का है।	*This is 50 rupees.*
आज मौसम कितना अच्छा है!	*How nice is the weather today!*

हिंदी में लिखिए *(Write in Hindi.)*

१. How many sisters do you *(formal)* have? _____

२. I have one sister. _____

३. How many cars do you *(informal)* have? _____

४. How much are these apples? _____

५. How expensive is the pear! _____

६. How beautiful is this building! _____

७. How much are the onions? _____

८. How much are the carrots? _____

Animals and the senses
जानवर व इंद्रियाँ

Wild and domestic animals of India and Hindi fables • भारत व हिंदी कथाओं के जंगली और पालतू जानवर

Most animals, insects, and birds in Hindi have one gender. If two genders are in use, they are also given below. These are singular forms and will change based on the gender and number.

alligator	घड़ियाल (*m.*)
ant, insect	कीड़ा (*m.*), मकोड़ा (*m.*), कीड़ी (*f.*), चींटी (*f.*)
bat	चमगादड़ (*m.*)
bear	भालू (*m.*)
bull	बैल (*m.*)
butterfly	तितली (*f.*)
calf	बछड़ा (*m.*), बछड़ी (*f.*)
camel	ऊँट (*m.*), ऊँटनी (*f.*)
cat	बिल्ला (*m.*), बिल्ली (*f.*)
cheetah	चीता (*m.*)
cobra	भुजंग (*m.*)
cow	गाय (*f.*)
crab	केंकड़ा (*m.*)
crane	सारस (*m.*)
crocodile	मगरमच्छ (*m.*)
crow	कौआ (*m.*)
deer	हिरन (*m.*), *doe* हिरनी (*f.*)
dog	कुत्ता (*m.*), *bitch* कुतिया (*f.*)
donkey	गधा (*m.*), गधी (*f.*)
duck	बतख (*f.*)
eagle	चील (*f.*)

earthworm	केंचुआ (*m.*)
elephant	गज (*m.*), हाथी (*m.*), हथिनी (*f.*)
firefly	जुगनु (*m.*)
fish	मछली (*f.*)
fox	लोमड़ी (*f.*)
frog, toad	मेंढक (*m.*)
goat	बकरा (*m.*), बकरी (*f.*)
grasshopper	टिड्डा (*m.*)
hippopotamus	दरयाई घोड़ा (*m.*)
honey bee	मधुमक्खी (*f.*)
horse	घोड़ा (*m.*), *mare* घोड़ी (*f.*)
housefly	मक्खी (*f.*)
hyena	सियार (*m.*)
jackal	गीदड़ (*m.*), गीदड़ी (*f.*)
lamb	मेमना (*m.*)
lion	शेर, सिंह (*m.*)
lizard	छिपकली (*f.*)
locust	टिड्डी (*f.*)
monkey	बन्दर (*m.*), बंदरिया (*f.*)
mosquito	मच्छर (*m.*)
mule	खच्चर, टट्टू (*m.*)
owl	उल्लू (*m.*)
panther, leopard	तेंदुआ (*m.*)
parrot	तोता (*m.*)
peacock	मोर (*m.*), मोरनी (*f.*)
pig	सूअर (*m.*)
pigeon	कबूतर (*m.*), कबूतरी (*f.*)
python	अजगर (*m.*)
rabbit	खरगोश (*m.*)
rat, mouse	चूहा (*m.*), चुहिया (*f.*)
rhinoceros	गैंडा (*m.*)
rooster	मुर्गा (*m.*), *hen* मुर्गी (*f.*)
scorpion	बिच्छू (*m.*)
sheep	भेड़ (*m.*)
skunk	छछूंदर (*f.*)
snake	साँप (*m.*)

sparrow	चिड़िया (*f.*)
spider	मकड़ी (*f.*)
squirrel	गिलहरी (*f.*)
swan	हंस (m)
tiger	बाघ (*m.*)
tortoise, turtle	कछुआ (*m.*)
vulture	गिद्ध (*m.*)
wandering bull	सांड (*m.*)
water buffalo	भैंसा (*m.*), भैंस (*f.*)
wolf	भेड़िया (*m.*)

Cultural insight

In the Indian society, the following animals are used as derogatory terms:

उल्लू, गधा, कुत्ता, और कुतिया

In contrast, the following have a positive connotation:

शेर, हिरनी, और हंस

अभ्यास २१·१

Match the animal with the place it is most likely to be found.

१.	केंकड़ा	आसमान में
२.	अजगर	छत पर
३.	बिल्ली	पिंजरे में (in the cage)
४.	कबूतर	चिड़िया घर में
५.	केंचुआ	जंगल में
६.	गिलहरी	पानी में
७.	चील	रेस्तरां में
८.	चूहा	घर में
९.	मछली	बगीचे में
१०.	शेर	ज़मीन पर

ठीक या ग़लत? *Mark True or False.*

१.   उल्लू उड़ता (*flies*) है।   _____

२.   कुत्ता भौंकता (*barks*) है।   _____

३.   चूहा बिल्ली से नहीं डरता।   _____

४.   तितली रंग-बिरंगी होती है।   _____

५.   गाय दूध और संतरे का रस देती (*gives*) है।   _____

६.   मकड़ी जाल (*web*) बुनती है।   _____

७.   मछली पानी में तैरती है।   _____

८.   मधुमक्खी शहद और लस्सी देती है।   _____

९.   मोर भारत का राष्ट्रीय पक्षी (*national bird*) है।   _____

१०. शेर दहाड़ता (*roars*) है।   _____

Parts of the body and the senses • शरीर के अंग व इंद्रियाँ

Below are parts of the body in both singular and plural forms.

ankle	टखना (*m. s.*), टखने (*m. pl.*)
arm	बाजू (*f. s.*), बाजुएँ (*f. pl.*)
armpit	बगल (*f. s.*), बगलें (*f. pl.*)
back	पीठ (*f. s.*)
breast	स्तन (*m. s.*)
buttock	नितंब (*m. s./pl.*)
calf	पिंडली (*f. s.*), पिंडलियाँ (*f. pl.*)
chest	छाती (*f. s.*)
chin	ठोड़ी (*f. s.*)
ear	कान (*m. s./pl.*)
elbow	कोहनी (*f. s.*), कोहनियाँ (*f. pl.*)
eye	आँख (*f.*), आँखें (*f. pl.*)
eyeball	आँख की पुतली (*f.*), आँख की पुतलियाँ (*f. pl.*)
eyebrow	भौंह (*f.*), भौंहें (*f. pl.*)
eyelash	पलक (*f. s.*), पलकें (*f. pl.*)
face	चेहरा (*m. s.*)

finger	उँगली (f. s.), उँगलियाँ (f. pl.)
forehead	माथा (m. s.)
gum	मसूड़ा (m. s.), मसूड़े (m. pl.)
hair	बाल (m. s./pl.)
hand	हाथ (m. s./pl.)
head	सिर (m. s./pl.)
heart	दिल, हृदय (m. s.)
heel	एड़ी (f. s.), एड़ियाँ (f. pl.)
hip	कूल्हा (m. s.)
jaw	जबड़ा (m. s.)
knee	घुटना (m. s.), घुटने (m. pl.)
leg	टाँग (f. s.), टाँगें (f. pl.)
lip	होंठ (m. s./pl.)
mouth	मुँह (m. s./pl.)
nail	नाखुन (m. s.), नाखुन (m. pl.)
navel	नाभि (f. s.)
neck	गर्दन (f. s.)
nose	नाक (m. and f. s./pl.)
nostril	नथुना (m. s.), नथुने (m. pl.)
palm	हथेली (f. s.), हथेलियाँ (f. pl.)
shoulder	कंधा (m. s.), कंधे (m. pl.)
skin	त्वचा (f. s./pl.)
sole	तलवा (m. s.), तलवे (m. pl.)
stomach	पेट (m. s./pl.)
temple	कनपट्टी (f.), कनपट्टियाँ (f. pl.)
thigh	जाँघ (f. s.), जाँघें (f. pl.)
throat	गला (m. s.)
thumb	अंगूठा (m. s.), अंगूठे (m. pl.)
toe	पैर की उँगली (f. s.), पैर की उँगलियाँ (f. pl.)
big toe	पैर का अंगूठा (m. s.), पैर के अंगूठे (m. pl.)
tongue	जीभ (f. s.)
tooth	दाँत (m. s./pl.)
waist	कमर (f. s.)
wrist	कलाई (f. s.), कलाइयाँ (f. pl.)

Some verbs used with the body and senses

हम आँखों से देखते हैं।	*We see from the eyes.*
हम पलकें झपकते हैं।	*We bat our eyelashes.*
हम नाक से सूँघते हैं।	*We smell from our nose.*
हम कानों से सुनते हैं।	*We hear from our ears.*
हम मुँह से बोलते और खाते हैं।	*We speak and eat from our mouth.*
हम दाँतों से चबाते हैं।	*We chew with our teeth.*
हम जीभ से स्वाद लेते हैं।	*We taste with our tongue.*
हम हाथों से छूते हैं।	*We touch with our hands.*
हम नाखुन काटते हैं।	*We cut our nails.*
हम टाँगों से चलते हैं।	*We walk with our legs.*

अभ्यास
२१·३

हिंदी को उसके अंग्रेज़ी अर्थ से मिलाइए (*Match the Hindi with its meaning in English.*)

१.	छोटे काले बाल	white teeth
२.	ख़ूबसूरत चेहरा	long fingers
३.	बड़ा माथा	long eyelashes
४.	लाल कनपट्टियाँ	short black hair
५.	गहरी भूरी आँखें	pink lips
६.	लंबी पलकें	big forehead
७.	गुलाबी होंठ	dark brown eyes
८.	सफ़ेद दाँत	beautiful face
९.	चौड़े कंधे	wide shoulders
१०.	पतली उँगलियाँ	red temples

अभ्यास
२१·४

ठीक या ग़लत? *Mark True or False.*

१. डकोटा फ़ैनिंग के बाल सुनहरे और लंबे हैं। _____

२. भालू की पाँच टाँगें होती हैं। _____

३. कछुए की पीठ सख़्त होती है। _____

४. जे लैनो की ठोड़ी लंबी और टेढ़ी है। _____

५. पिनोकियो का नाक बहुत छोटा है। _____

६. मिकी माऊस के कई कान हैं। _____

७. गिलहरी के हाथ बहुत बड़े होते हैं। _____

८. मगरमच्छ का एक दांत होता है। _____

अभ्यास
२१·५

Use the model below and write five sentences in Hindi describing your mother.

मेरी माता जी ख़ूबसूरत हैं। उनके बाल छोटे और भूरे हैं। उनकी आँखें हरी हैं। उनकी नाक पतली है। उनकी गर्दन लंबी है। उनके हाथ और पैर साफ़ हैं।

Verbs with postposition को: Bodily ailments • शारीरिक परेशानियाँ

Like hunger and thirst, bodily ailments are also viewed as a physical experience. The sense of having an ailment is expressed using verbs with postposition को:

to have a stomachache	को पेट में दर्द (*m.*) होना
to have a headache	को सिर में दर्द (*m.*) होना
to have a fever	को बुखार (*m.*) होना
to have a cold	को ज़ुकाम (*m.*) होना
to have the flu	को नज़ला (*m.*) होना
to have weakness	को कमज़ोरी होना
to sneeze	को छींक (*f.*) आना
to cough	को खाँसी (*f.*) आना
to vomit	को उल्टी (*f.*) आना
to sweat	को पसीना आना
to be dizzy	को चक्कर आना
to have dysentery	को दस्त (*m.*) लगना, पेचिश (*f.*) होना
to have constipation	को कब्ज़ होना
to have an itch	को खुजली (*f.*) होना
to have a swelling	को सूजन (*f.*) होना
to have an injury	को चोट (*f.*) लगना

हिन्दी में लिखिए *(Write in Hindi.)*

१. He has a cough. _____

२. She sneezes. _____

३. They have an itch. _____

४. We have a cold. _____

५. You *(formal)* have a fever. _____

६. I have the flu. _____

७. You *(informal)* have a swelling. _____

Compound postpositions • अव्यय/अविकारी शब्द

Beyond simple postpositions, Hindi has many compound postpositions. *Compound* in this case means that these postpositions consist of two words and one of these words is always either के or की. Like all postpositions, compound postpositions require the use of the oblique case of nouns, adjectives, and possessives.

about	के बारे में
above, on top of	के ऊपर
across	के पार
adjacent to	की बगल में
after	के बाद
all around, on all sides	के इर्दगिर्द/चारों ओर
around, in the neighborhood of	के आसपास
aside from	के इलावा, अतिरिक्त
at the edge of	के किनारे पर
because of	के कारण, की वजह से
before, first	के/से पहले
behind, at the back of	के पीछे
below, underneath	के नीचे
compared to, in comparison to	की तुलना में, के मुक़ाबले में
during	के दौरान
except	के सिवा
facing, opposite of	के सामने
for	के लिए
in front of	के आगे
in the middle of, in between	के बीच में

inside	के अंदर
instead of	की बजाय
like	की तरह
near, nearby	के पास, नज़दीक
outside	के बाहर
owing to, out of	के मारे
toward, in the direction of	की ओर, तरफ़
with	के साथ
without	के बिना

अभ्यास

२१·७

Fill in the compound postposition.

१. in front of   _____

२. facing, opposite of   _____

३. behind, at the back of   _____

४. above, on top of   _____

५. below, underneath   _____

६. in the middle of, in between   _____

७. during   _____

८. about   _____

९. near, nearby   _____

१०. after   _____

अभ्यास

२१·८

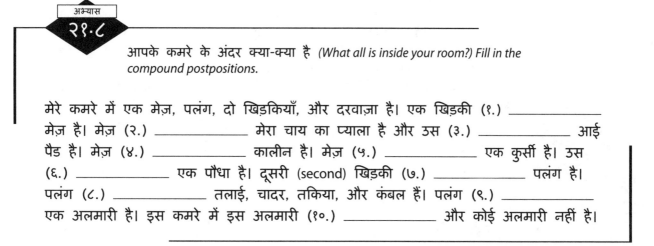

आपके कमरे के अंदर क्या-क्या है (*What all is inside your room?*) Fill in the compound postpositions.

मेरे कमरे में एक मेज़, पलंग, दो खिड़कियाँ, और दरवाज़ा है। एक खिड़की (१.) _____ मेज़ है। मेज़ (२.) _____ मेरा चाय का प्याला है और उस (३.) _____ आई पैड है। मेज़ (४.) _____ कालीन है। मेज़ (५.) _____ एक कुर्सी है। उस (६.) _____ एक पौधा है। दूसरी (second) खिड़की (७.) _____ पलंग है। पलंग (८.) _____ तलाई, चादर, तकिया, और कंबल हैं। पलंग (९.) _____ एक अलमारी है। इस कमरे में इस अलमारी (१०.) _____ और कोई अलमारी नहीं है।

The past tense
भूतकाल

The imperative • आग्यार्थ विधि

The imperative form is used to make requests or give commands. As such, it is related to the pronoun *you*. This means that it has different forms for each of the three types of *you* in Hindi, आप, तुम, and तू, indicating varying degrees of formality.

Similar to other verb conjugations, the imperative form is constructed by first isolating the verb stem. If the verb stem ends in a consonant, then the diacritic mark for इए is added as a suffix to the verb stem for आप; the diacritic mark for ओ is added as a suffix to the verb stem for तुम; and the verb stem itself is used for तू.

Look at these examples for the verbs पढ़ना, लिखना, और देखना:

	पढ़ना	लिखना	देखना
आप (*formal*)	पढ़िए	लिखिए	देखिए
तुम (*informal*)	पढ़ो	लिखो	देखो
तुम (*informal*)	पढ़ना	लिखना	देखना
तू (*informal*)	पढ़	लिख	देख

The polite imperative form with आप (*formal*) translates into a request that means "please do something."

The first imperative form with तुम (*informal*) form and तू (*informal*) translates into "do something."

The second तुम form with the infinitive verb is a request that does not have to be fulfilled immediately. There is usually a time lag associated with this request; it roughly translates as "be sure to do that when you can."

If the verb stem ends in आ, such as in the verbs खाना = खा, जाना = जा, आना = आ, then, as shown below, the इए and ओ suffixes are spelled out (instead of being attached as diacritic marks).

	खाना	जाना	आना
आप	खाइए	जाइए	आइए
तुम	खाओ	जाओ	आओ
तुम	खाना	जाना	आना
तू	खा	जा	आ

A handful of verbs have irregular imperative forms, such as करना (*to do*), लेना (*to take*), देना (*to give*), and और पीना (*to drink*).

	करना	लेना	देना	पीना
आप	कीजिए	लीजिए	दीजिए	पीजिए
तुम	करो	लो	दो	पीओ
तुम	करना	लेना	देना	पीना
तू	कर	ले	दे	पी

अंदर आइए।	*Please come in.*
बैठिए।	*Please sit.*
यह सोमवार को लेना।	*Take this on Monday.*
बाहर जाओ।	*Go outside.*
यह किताब मुझे दो।	*Give this book to me.*

अभ्यास
२२·१

हिंदी में लिखिए (*Write in Hindi.*)

१. Please drive this car. _____

२. Do my work tomorrow. _____

३. Ask him. _____

४. Please turn on the light. _____

५. Please close the door. _____

६. Cook the food. _____

Some more useful verbs

to rest, relax	आराम करना	to wear	पहनना
to try	कोशिश करना	to use	इस्तेमाल करना
to begin	शुरु करना	to wash	धोना
to finish	खत्म करना	to know	जानना, मालूम होना, पता होना
to clean	साफ़ करना	to laugh	हँसना
to respond, answer	जवाब देना	to cry	रोना
to arrive	पहुँचना	to tell	बताना
to buy	खरीदना	to open	खोलना
to catch	पकड़ना	to close	बंद करना
to call (not on the phone)	बुलाना	to return	लौटना, वापिस आना

हिन्दी में लिखिए (*Write in Hindi.*)

१. Wash the car. _____

२. Please try. _____

३. Catch the bus! _____

४. You rest. _____

५. Please start the work today. _____

६. Clean the room! _____

७. Please arrive in Delhi by tomorrow. _____

८. Laugh every day. _____

९. Open the door! _____

१०. Please close the door. _____

Use of मत, सिर्फ़, और भी for negatives and emphasis

Instead of नहीं (*no*), the most common way to negate the imperative form is by using the word मत (*do not*). Like नहीं, it is placed before the verb to negate the action.

खिड़की मत खोलो।	*Do not open the window.*
सीढ़ियाँ मत लो।	*Do not take the stairs.*

The word सिर्फ़ means *only* and is used to emphasize a particular noun or verb:

सिर्फ़ यह मेज़ खरीदिए।	*Buy only this table.*
सिर्फ़ पाँच दिन स्कूल जाना।	*Go to school only five days.*

The particle भी means *also* or *too* and is used *after* what needs to be emphasized:

इस गाड़ी को भी देखो।	*Look at this car too.*
मैं भी यह पसंद करती हूँ।	*I also like this.*
उस को तुम से भी प्यार है।	*He loves you too.*

Note: Unlike English, sentences in Hindi never begin with *also*. भी is only placed after what is intended to be emphasized.

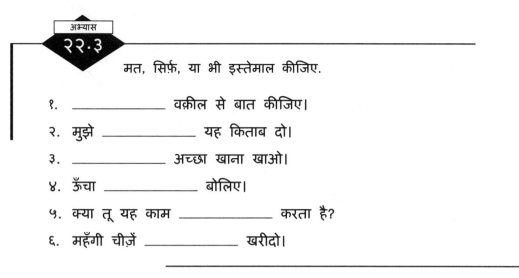

मत, सिर्फ़, या भी इस्तेमाल कीजिए.

१. _____ वक़ील से बात कीजिए।

२. मुझे _____ यह किताब दो।

३. _____ अच्छा खाना खाओ।

४. ऊँचा _____ बोलिए।

५. क्या तू यह काम _____ करता है?

६. महँगी चीज़ें _____ खरीदो।

Travel and directions • यात्रा और दिशाएँ

to take a domestic flight	घरेलू उड़ान लेना
to take an international flight	अंतराष्ट्रीय उड़ान लेना
flight number	उड़ान नम्बर
gate number	द्वार नम्बर
to show the passport	पासपोर्ट दिखाना
to show the visa	वीज़ा दिखाना
to show the boarding pass	बोर्डिंग पास दिखाना
to have the security check done	सुरक्षा जाँच करवाना
luggage	सामान
to check in	चैक इन करना
immigration	आप्रवास
arrival	आगमन
departure	प्रस्थान
to rent a car or taxi	किराए की गाड़ी या टैक्सी लेना
driver	चालक
road	सड़क
way	रास्ता
highway	राज मार्ग
where	कहाँ, किधर
here	यहाँ, इधर
there	वहाँ, उधर
where, there	जहाँ, जिधर
sign	चिन्ह
east	पूर्व
west	पश्चिम
south	दक्षिण
north	उत्तर

at the traffic light	लाल बत्ती पर
to turn left	दाएं मुड़ना
to turn right	बाएं मुड़ना
to park	पार्क करना
to stop	रुकना
to drive	चलाना
to fill gas (in the car)	पैट्रोल भरना
speed bump	गति अवरोधक
speed limit	गति सीमा
intersection	चौराहा
roundabout	गोलचक्कर
exit ramp	निकास ढलान
for a car to break down	गाड़ी ख़राब होना
to change the tire	पहिया बदलना
Can you help me?	क्या आप मेरी मदद कर सकते हैं?
insurance	बीमा
mechanic	मिस्त्री

अभ्यास
२२·४

अंग्रेज़ी को उसके हिंदी अर्थ से मिलाइए (Match the English with its Hindi meaning.)

१.	What is the flight number?	आप के पास बीमा है?
२.	Where is the security check?	यह मेरा सामान है।
३.	This is my luggage.	मैं एक गाड़ी किराए पर लेना चाहता हूँ।
४.	This is not my luggage.	यह मेरा सामान नहीं है।
५.	I want to rent a car.	सुरक्षा जाँच किधर है?
६.	Go straight.	यहाँ पर पार्क करो।
७.	Turn right at the traffic light.	क्या आसपास कोई पैट्रोल पम्प है?
८.	Park here.	सीधा चलो।
९.	Stop here.	लाल बत्ती पर बाएं मुड़ो।
१०.	Is there a gas station nearby?	मेरा उड़ान नम्बर क्या है?
११.	Turn left at the intersection.	आसपास कोई मिस्त्री की दुकान है?
१२.	Do you have insurance?	यहाँ रुको।
१३.	Is there a mechanic shop nearby?	चौराहे पर दाएं मुड़ो।

हिन्दी में लिखिए *(Write in Hindi.)*

१. Can you help me? _____

२. I want to change the tire. _____

३. What is the gate number for this flight? _____

४. Where is Lisa Inn? _____

५. Take this exit ramp. _____

Past indefinite tense • सामान्य भूतकाल

The past indefinite tense is constructed by replacing the है and हैं from the present indefinite tense with था *(m. s.)*, थे *(m. pl.)*, थी *(f. s.)*, and थीं *(f. pl.)*.

I used to go	मैं जाता था। *(m. s.)*
I used to go	मैं जाती थी। *(f. s.)*
you (informal) used to go	तू जाता था। *(m. s.)*
you (informal) used to go	तू जाती थी। *(f. s.)*
you (informal) used to go	तुम जाते थे। *(m. s.)*
you (informal) used to go	तुम जाती थीं। *(f. s.)*
he/it used to go	यह/वह जाता था। *(m. s.)*
she/it used to go	यह/वह जाती थी। *(f. s.)*
you (formal) used to go	आप जाते थे। *(m. pl.)*
you (formal) used to go	आप जाती थीं। *(f. pl.)*
we used to go	हम जाते थे। *(m. pl.)*
we used to go	हम जाती थीं। *(f. pl.)*
they/these/those used to go	ये/वे जाते थे। *(m. pl.)*
they/these/those used to go	ये वे जाती थीं। *(f. pl.)*

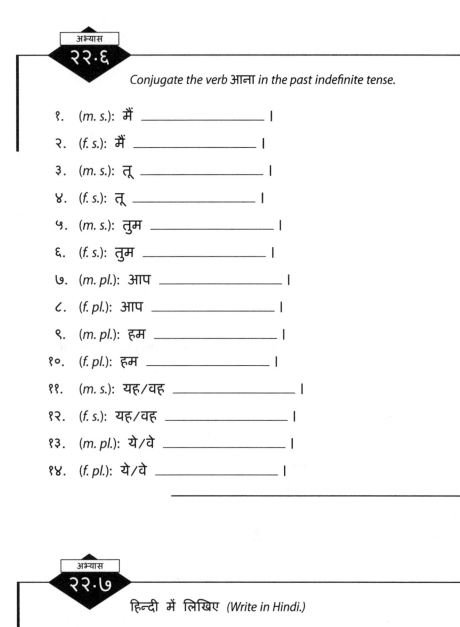

Conjugate the verb आना *in the past indefinite tense.*

१. (*m. s.*): मैं _____ |

२. (*f. s.*): मैं _____ |

३. (*m. s.*): तू _____ |

४. (*f. s.*): तू _____ |

५. (*m. s.*): तुम _____ |

६. (*f. s.*): तुम _____ |

७. (*m. pl.*): आप _____ |

८. (*f. pl.*): आप _____ |

९. (*m. pl.*): हम _____ |

१०. (*f. pl.*): हम _____ |

११. (*m. s.*): यह/वह _____ |

१२. (*f. s.*): यह/वह _____ |

१३. (*m. pl.*): ये/वे _____ |

१४. (*f. pl.*): ये/वे _____ |

हिन्दी में लिखिए *(Write in Hindi.)*

१. I used to watch TV every day. _____

२. She used to relax on Sundays. _____

३. We used to laugh. _____

४. They used to talk to us. _____

५. It used to be cheap. _____

Reading practice • पढ़ने का अभ्यास

For added practice, read this recipe for the popular warm Indian Masala Chai that uses the imperative form.

<u>मसाला चाय कैसे बनाते हैं?</u>

१. एक लौंग, कुछ इलायची के दाने, थोड़ी दालचीनी, और अदरक पीसिए।

२. एक कप पानी में इन सब चीजों को डालिए और उबालिए।

३. एक चुटकी काली मिर्च भी डालिए।

४. आधा कप दूध और स्वाद के अनुसार चीनी डालिए।

५. एक चम्मच चाय पत्ती मिलाइए और दोबारा उबालिए।

६. फिर, कप या केतली में छानिए और पीजिए।

Vocabulary

लौंग	cloves	आधा	half
इलायची के दाने	cardamom seeds	स्वाद के अनुसार	according to taste
दालचीनी	cinnamon	चीनी	sugar
अदरक	ginger	चम्मच	spoon
पीसना	to grind	चाय पत्ती	tea leaves
सब	all	मिलाना	to mix
डालना	to put	दोबारा	again
उबालना	to boil	केतली	kettle
चुटकी	a pinch	छानना	to strain
काली मिर्च	black pepper		

Translate the recipe into English.

_____

_____

_____

_____

_____

_____

THE CONTINUOUS
AND FUTURE TENSES
पाठ ८: अपूर्ण व भविष्य काल

Grammar

Telling time
Interrogative word (प्रश्नार्थक शब्द) कब
Interrogative word (प्रश्नार्थक शब्द) कौन
Present and past continuous tenses
The future tense

Vocabulary

Time-related phrases and adverbs
Ordinal numbers
Seasons, environment, and the weather
Clothes and accessories
Some more useful verbs

Culture

Cultural notes/insights
Reading practice: Hindi words in English

Time
समय/वक्त

Telling time • समय बताना

time	समय (*m.*), वक्त (*m.*)
watch, clock	घड़ी (*f.*)
year	वर्ष (*m.*), साल (*m.*)
month	मास (*m.*), महीना (*m.*)
week	ससाह (*m.*), हफ़्ता (*m.*)
hour	घंटा (*m.*)
minute	मिनट (*m.*)
second	क्षण (*m.*), पल (*m.*)
to chime, to sound	बजना
in the morning	सुबह (*f.*), सवेरा (*m.*), प्रातःकाल (*m.*)
in the afternoon	दोपहर (*f.*) को
in the evening	शाम (*f.*), सायंकाल (*m.*) को
at night	रात (*f.*), रात्री (*f.*) को

In Hindi, there are several ways to ask "What time is it?"

कितने बजे हैं?	*How many chimes?*
क्या बजा है?	*What has chimed?*
क्या समय हुआ (है)?	*What time is it?*
क्या वक्त हुआ (है)?	*What time is it?*

The response "It is _____ o'clock" is made using the verb बजना.

एक बजा है एक बजे हैं।	*It is one o'clock.*
दो बजे हैं।	*It is two o'clock.*

Special words are used for certain times, such as:

1:30	डेढ़
2:30	ढाई
A quarter after or one and a quarter	सवा
One and a half (except 1:30 and 2:30)	साढ़े
A quarter to	पौने
1:15	सवा एक बजा है or सवा एक बजे हैं।
1:30	डेढ़ बजा है or डेढ़ बजे हैं।
1:45	पौने दो बजे हैं।
2:00	दो बजे हैं।
2:15	सवा दो बजे हैं।
2:30	ढाई बजे हैं।
2:45	पौने तीन बजे हैं।
3:00	तीन बजे हैं।
3:15	सवा तीन बजे हैं।
3:30	साढ़े तीन बजे हैं।
3:45	पौने चार बजे हैं।

अभ्यास
२३·१

हिंदी में लिखिए *(Write in Hindi.)*

१. It is 4:00. _____

२. 6:15 _____

३. 8:15 _____

४. 3:30 _____

५. 5:30 _____

६. 1:30 _____

७. 2:30 _____

८. 9:45 _____

९. 7:45 _____

१०. 10:00 _____

The following expressions are used to indicate different parts of the day or am and pm.

सुबह के	of the morning (am)
दोपहर के	of the afternoon (pm)
शाम के	of the evening (pm)
रात के	of the night (pm)
आधी रात	midnight

When it is necessary to specify the particular part of the day along with the time, these expressions are generally placed at the beginning of the sentence. For example:

It is 9:00 am.	सुबह के नौ बजे हैं।
It is 12:00 pm.	दोपहर के बारह बजे हैं।
It is midnight.	आधी रात है।

For the times in between, other constructions are used. For instance:

It is about to be 5 o'clock.	पाँच बजने वाले हैं।
It is 10 minutes after 5:00.	पाँच बजकर १० मिनट हैं।
It is 10 minutes to 5:00.	पाँच बजने में १० मिनट हैं।
It is exactly 5 o'clock.	ठीक पाँच बजे हैं।
It is about/approximately 5 o'clock.	लगभग/तकरीबन पाँच बजे हैं।

Note: As in English, one can also state the numerical or digital time, such as 11:55.

अभ्यास

२३·२

हिंदी में लिखिए *(Write in Hindi.)*

१. It is 7:00 pm. _____

२. 11:00 pm. _____

३. 8:00 am. _____

४. 9:00 am. _____

५. 12:00 pm. _____

६. It is about to be 4 o'clock. _____

७. It is 20 minutes after 6. _____

८. It is 40 minutes to 5. _____

९. It is exactly 3 o'clock. _____

१०. It is about/approximately 2 o'clock. _____

Time-related phrases and adverbs • समय-संबंधी पद-बंध एवं क्रिया-विशेषण

at this/that time	इस/उस समय
this week/month/year	इस सप्ताह, महीने, साल
next week/month/year	अगले सप्ताह, महीने, साल
last week/month/year	पिछले सप्ताह, महीने, साल
two weeks ago	दो हफ़्ते पहले
this morning	आज सुबह
this afternoon	आज दोपहर को
this evening	आज शाम को
tonight	आज रात को
every night	हर रात को
now	अब
right now	अभी
today	आज
yesterday	कल
tomorrow	कल
the day after tomorrow/yesterday	परसों
all the time	हर समय
all day (long)	सारा दिन, दिन भर
all night (long)	सारी रात, रात भर
during the day	दिन के दौरान
before	पहले
after/later	बाद में
often	अक्सर
never	कभी नहीं
sometimes (also, from time to time)	कभी-कभी
always	हमेशा
early	जल्दी
quickly	जल्दी से
late	देर से
first of all	सबसे पहले
for the first time	पहली बार (*f.*)
for the last time	आखिरी बार (*f.*)
time and again	बार-बार, घड़ी-घड़ी

अभ्यास
२३·३

हिंदी में लिखिए *(Write in Hindi.)*

१. this week _____

२. next week _____

३. last week _____

४. this morning _____

५. tonight _____

६. now _____

७. yesterday/tomorrow _____

८. during the day _____

९. often _____

१०. never _____

११. sometimes (also, from time to time) _____

१२. always _____

१३. early _____

१४. late _____

१५. first of all _____

अभ्यास
२३·४

Use the following passage about Sanjay's daily activities on a Sunday as a model and write about your daily activities on Sunday.

हर हफ़्ते संजय को सिर्फ़ रविवार की छुट्टी (holiday) होती है। अक्सर उस दिन वह देर से उठता है। वह लगभग साढ़े ग्यारह या पौने बारह बजे उठता है। फिर, वह दाँत साफ़ करता है, नहाता है, और नाश्ता (breakfast) बनाता है। इन कामों को वह हर रोज़ ठीक एक घंटे में करता है पर रविवार को कभी-कभी वह ज़्यादा समय लेता है। नाश्ते के बाद वह दो दस से तीन दस तक बाहर घूमने जाता है। फिर, दोपहर को चार बजे से पहले वह दोपहर का खाना खाता है और उसके साथ सारे हफ़्ते की डाक पढ़ता है। तकरीबन छः बजे वह टी. वी. देखता है। कभी-कभी, एक फ़िल्म भी देखता है। हर शाम को वह व्यायाम (exercise) करता है। रात को वह समय पर सोना पसन्द करता है। वह लगभग दस बजे सोता है।

_____

_____

_____

_____

_____

Interrogative word (प्रश्नार्थक शब्द) कब

Interrogative word कब means *when* and, as it ends in a consonant, it does not change with the gender and number of what is inquired about.

आपका जन्मदिन (*m.*) कब था?	*When was your birthday?*
पंकज की शादी (*f.*) कब है?	*When is Pankaj's wedding?*

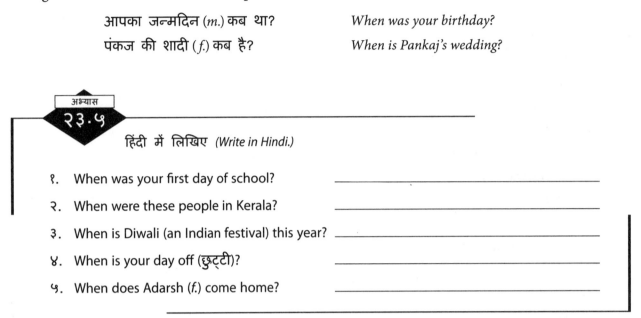

अभ्यास
२३·५

हिंदी में लिखिए *(Write in Hindi.)*

१. When was your first day of school? _____

२. When were these people in Kerala? _____

३. When is Diwali (an Indian festival) this year? _____

४. When is your day off (छुट्टी)? _____

५. When does Adarsh (*f.*) come home? _____

Ordinal numbers • क्रम संख्याएँ

Aside from the first six, the rest of the ordinal numbers are formed by adding the suffix -वाँ to the spelling of the cardinal numbers you learned earlier.

first	पहला	*twelfth*	बारहवाँ
second	दूसरा	*thirteenth*	तेरहवाँ
third	तीसरा	*fourteenth*	चौदहवाँ
fourth	चौथा	*fifteenth*	पंद्रहवाँ
fifth	पाँचवाँ	*sixteenth*	सोलहवाँ
sixth	छटा	*seventeenth*	सत्रहवाँ
seventh	सातवाँ	*eighteenth*	अठारहवाँ
eighth	आठवाँ	*nineteenth*	उन्नीसवाँ
ninth	नौवाँ	*twentieth*	बीसवाँ
tenth	दसवाँ	*hundredth*	सौवाँ
eleventh	ग्यारहवाँ		

However, as the suffix -वाँ ends with the vowel आ, it will change based on the number and gender of the noun being discussed. For example,

first day	पहला दिन (*m.*)
first night	पहली रात (*f.*)
in the first few months	पहले कुछ महीनों (*m. pl.*) में

हिंदी में लिखिए *(Write in Hindi.)*

१. the first day of school   _____

२. second wife   _____

३. the third eye   _____

४. fourth place   _____

५. seventh heaven   _____

६. sixteenth candle   _____

७. sixtieth birthday   _____

८. hundredth time   _____

The continuous tense
अपूर्ण काल

Interrogative word (प्रश्नार्थक शब्द) कौन

The interrogative word कौन means *who* and, like कब, it does not modify based on the gender and number of the noun.

यह लड़की कौन है?	*Who is this girl?*
वे लोग कौन हैं?	*Who are those people?*

अभ्यास २४·१

ये लोग कौन हैं? *(Guess who?)*

१. इस आदमी के बाल स्लेटी हैं और यह एक प्रसिद्ध वैग्यानिक (famous scientist) था।

२. इस आदमी के बाल छोटे व काले हैं और यह इस समय अमरीका का राष्ट्रपति है।

३. इस औरत के लाल बाल थे और यह रिकी रकार्डो की पत्नी थी।

४. यह औरत एक अभिनेत्री है और इसका पहला नाम मैरिल है।

५. यह बार-बार ई. टी. फ़ोन होम कहता था।

Seasons, environment, and the weather • ऋतुएँ, पर्यावरण, और मौसम

Seasons • ऋतुएँ

summer	गर्मी (*f.*), ग्रीष्म (*f.*)
winter	सर्दी (*f.*), जाड़ा (*m.*)
fall/autumn	शरद (*m.*), पतझड़ (*f.*)
spring	बसन्त (*m.*), बहार (*f.*)
monsoon	मानसून (*m.*)

174

आज मौसम कैसा है?   *How is the weather today?*

आज थोड़ी गर्मी है।   *It is a little hot today.*

कल मौसम कैसा था?   *How was the weather yesterday?*

कल सर्दी थी।   *It was cold yesterday.*

The environment • पर्यावरण

sea	सागर (*m.*)		valley	घाटी (*f.*)
ocean	महासागर (*m.*)		glacier	हिमनद (*m.*)
island	द्वीप (*m.*)		river	नदी (*f.*)
peninsula	प्रायद्वीप (*m.*)		lake	झील (*f.*)
continent	महाद्वीप (*m.*)		waterfall	झरना (*m.*)
subcontinent	उपमहाद्वीप (*m.*)		forest	जंगल (*m.*)
mountain	पहाड़ (*m.*), पर्वत (*m.*)		desert	रेगिस्तान (*m.*)

Weather and natural disasters • मौसम और प्राकृतिक दुर्घटनाएँ

for the snow to fall	हिमपात (*m.*) होना
to rain	बरसात (*f.*) होना
to flood	बाढ़ (*f.*) आना
for a hailstorm to come	ओले पड़ना
to become cloudy	बादल बनना
to thunder	बादल गरजना
for lightening to strike	बिजली गिरना
to be windy	हवा चलना
to be stormy	तूफ़ान आना
for a tornado to come	बवंडर आना
for a hurricane to come	चक्रवात आना
to be foggy	धुंध होना
to be sunny	धूप होना
to be shady	छांव होना
for a volcano to erupt	ज्वालामुखी फटना
for a landslide to happen	भूस्लखन होना
for an earthquake to come	भूकंप आना
for an avalanche to happen	हिमस्लखन होना

अंग्रेज़ी और हिंदी अर्थ को मिलाइए। *(Match the English and Hindi meanings.)*

१.	summer	हवा चलना
२.	winter	मानसून
३.	autumn	छांव होना
४.	spring	धुंध होना
५.	monsoon	सर्दी, जाड़ा
६.	for the snowfall to happen	धूप होना
७.	to rain	भूकंप आना
८.	to be windy	गर्मी, ग्रीष्म
९.	to be foggy	बसन्त, बहार
१०.	to be sunny	हिमपात होना
११.	to be shady	शरद, पतझड़
१२.	for an earthquake to come	बरसात आना

Fill in the blanks.

१. उत्तर अमरीका एक _____ है।

२. भारत एक _____ है।

३. फूल _____ के मौसम में खिलते हैं।

४. हिमालय एक बहुत ऊँचा _____ है।

५. भारत में गंगा एक _____ है।

६. राजस्थान सहारा की तरह एक _____ है।

७. नायैग्रा फ़ाल्स एक _____ है।

८. बादल बनते हैं और फ़िर _____ आती है।

९. बादल गरजते हैं और _____ गिरती है।

१०. हवा चलती है और _____ आता है।

Present and past continuous tense • अपूर्ण वर्तमान व भूत काल

The present continuous tense consists of taking the verb stem of the verb and adding another verb रहना to it, along with the present tense of होना that is normally there at the end of a sentence. The verb रहना communicates the sense of things being in motion or continuous. The important thing to note in continuous tenses is that the verb stem of the original verb is there, but does not change, only the verb stem of रहना gets conjugated.

Here is an example with the verb आना:

I am coming	मैं आ रहा हूँ। (*m. s.*)
I am coming	मैं आ रही हूँ। (*f. s.*)
you (informal) *are coming*	तू आ रहा है। (*m. s.*)
you (informal) *are coming*	तू आ रही है। (*f. s.*)
you (informal) *are coming*	तुम आ रहे हो। (*m. s.*)
you (informal) *are coming*	तुम आ रही हो। (*f. s.*)
you (formal) *are coming*	आप आ रहे हैं। (*m. pl.*)
you (formal) *are coming*	आप आ रही हैं। (*f. pl.*)
he/it is coming	यह, वह आ रहा है। (*m. s.*)
she/it is coming	यह, वह आ रही है। (*f. s.*)
we are coming	हम आ रहे हैं। (*m. pl.*)
we are coming	हम आ रही हैं। (*f. pl.*)
they/these/those are coming	ये, वे आ रहे हैं। (*m. pl.*)
they/these/those are coming	ये, वे आ रही हैं। (*f. pl.*)

The past continuous tense works the same way. Take the verb stem and add the verb रहना and end with the past tense of होना: था, थी, थे, थीं.

Here is an example with the verb चलना:

I was walking	मैं चल रहा था। (*m. s.*)
I was walking	मैं चल रही थी। (*f. s.*)
you (informal) *were walking*	तू चल रहा था। (*m. s.*)
you (informal) *were walking*	तू चल रही थी। (*f. s.*)
you (informal) *were walking*	तुम चल रहे थे। (*m. s.*)
you (informal) *were walking*	तुम चल रही थे। (*f. s.*)
you (formal) *were walking*	आप चल रहे थे। (*m. pl.*)
you (formal) *were walking*	आप चल रही थीं। (*f. pl.*)
he were/it was walking	यह, वह चल रहा था। (*m. s.*)
she were/it was walking	यह, वह चल रही थी। (*f. s.*)

we were walking	हम चल रहे थे। (*m. pl.*)
we were walking	हम चल रही थीं। (*f. pl.*)
they/these/those were walking	ये, वे चल रहे थे। (*m. pl.*)
they/these/those were walking	ये, वे चल रही थीं। (*f. pl.*)

अभ्यास
२४·४

Conjugate the verb जाना *in the present continuous tense and add the past continuous tense ending after the backslash.*

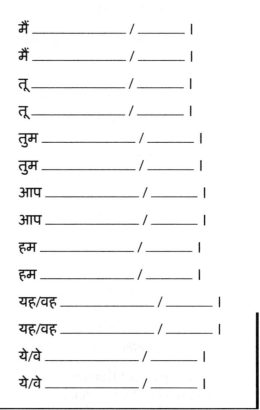

१.   (*m. s.*): I am/was going   मैं _____ / _____ ।

२.   (*f. s.*): I am/was going   मैं _____ / _____ ।

३.   (*m. s.*): you (*informal*) are/were going   तू_____ / _____ ।

४.   (*f. s.*): you (*informal*) are/were going   तू_____ / _____ ।

५.   (*m. s.*): you (*informal*) are/were going   तुम _____ / _____ ।

६.   (*f. s.*): you (*informal*) are/were going   तुम _____ / _____ ।

७.   (*m. pl.*): you (*formal*) are/were going   आप _____ / _____ ।

८.   (*f. pl.*): you (*formal*) are/were going   आप _____ / _____ ।

९.   (*m. pl.*): we are/were going   हम _____ / _____ ।

१०.   (*f. pl.*): we are/were going   हम _____ / _____ ।

११.   (*m. s.*): he/it are/were going   यह/वह _____ / _____ ।

१२.   (*f. s.*): she/it are/were going   यह/वह _____ / _____ ।

१३.   (*m. pl.*): they/those/these are/were going   ये/वे _____ / _____ ।

१४.   (*f. pl.*): they/those/these are/were going   ये/वे _____ / _____ ।

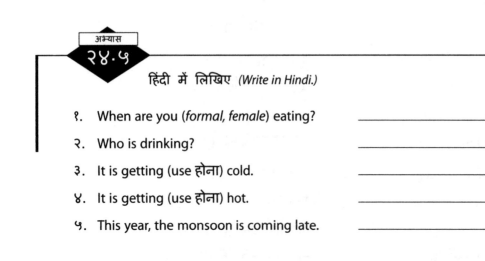

अभ्यास
२४·५

हिंदी में लिखिए *(Write in Hindi.)*

१.   When are you (*formal, female*) eating?   _____

२.   Who is drinking?   _____

३.   It is getting (use होना) cold.   _____

४.   It is getting (use होना) hot.   _____

५.   This year, the monsoon is coming late.   _____

178   THE CONTINUOUS AND FUTURE TENSES

६. It was raining. _____

७. It was becoming cloudy. _____

८. It is windy. _____

९. An earthquake is coming. _____

१०. Yesterday, it was foggy. _____

Some more useful verbs

to wear	पहनना
to take off	को उतारना
to respond	जवाब देना
to ask a question	से सवाल पूछना
to believe	विश्वास करना
to doubt	पर शक करना
to climb	पर चढ़ना
to get off	से उतरना
to fall	गिरना
to get up	उठ जाना
to feel	महसूस करना
to not care	परवाह नहीं करना
to forget	भूलना
to remember, memorize	याद करना
to sing	गाना
to think	सोचना

अभ्यास
२४·६

हिंदी में लिखिए *(Write in Hindi.)*

१. I (*female*) am asking you a question. _____

२. He is climbing the mountain. _____

३. She was getting off the bus. _____

४. We are feeling good. _____

५. The singer was singing. _____

६. They are thinking about this. _____

Future tense
भविष्यकाल

Clothes and accessories • कपड़े और सहायक वस्तुएँ

Much like Indian food, Indian clothes and accessories are world-renowned and a defining feature of the Indian culture. Indian women and men each have culturally-specific and well-defined sets of clothing.

Indian women's clothing • भारतीय महिलाओं के कपड़े

Traditional Indian women usually wear an outfit called a सूट that consists of a long shirt (कमीज़) topped with a sash (दुपट्टा) that is paired with a pant-like bottom (सलवार). Another common attire is the saree (साड़ी), a wrap-around dress tied around the waist over a petticoat and paired with a type of blouse. Either of these also serves as a professional attire. On special occasions, women wear a dress called लॅहगा, another type of top with a skirt.

The suit for women: सूट (*m.*)

- long shirt: कमीज़ (*f.*, the long shirt worn as part of the suit)
- sash: दुपट्टा (*m.*), चुन्नी (*f.*, the sash worn with a women's suit)
- bottom: सलवार (*f.*, bulky pant-like bottom worn with a suit), पजामी (*f.*, skinny pant-like bottom worn with a suit)

The wrap-around dress for women: साड़ी (*f.*)

- petticoat: पेटीकोट (*m.*, an underskirt worn under the saree)
- blouse: ब्लाऊज़ (*m.*, the top worn with the saree)

The top and skirt for women: लॅहगा (*m.*)

- skirt: घघरा (*m.*, a certain type of Indian skirt)
- top: चोली (*f.*, a top shirt worn with the ghaghrā)

modern skirt	स्कर्ट (*f.*)
evening gown	गाऊन (*m.*)
shawl	शॉल (*m.*)
sweater	स्वैटर (*m.*)
coat	कोट (*m.*)
T-shirt	टी शर्ट (*f.*)
jeans	जींस (*f.*)
scarf	गुलूबंद (*m.*)
belt	पेटी (*f.*)

prescription glasses	चश्मा (*m.*)
sunglasses	धूप का चश्मा (*m.*)
gloves	दस्ताने (*m. pl.*)
purse	पर्स (*m.*)
footwear (like flip-flops)	चप्पल
open-toe shoes	सैंडल

Indian men's clothing • भारतीय पुरुषों के कपड़े

Traditional Indian men's clothing consists of a long top (कुर्ता) and a pant-like bottom (पाजामा). Business attire is an Indian form of the Western business suit. On special occasions, a different type of a long top is worn (अचकन) with a tight pant-like bottom (पजामी).

casual long top	कुर्ता (*m.*)
pant-like bottom	पजामा (*m.*)
special long top	अचकन (*m.*)
tight pant-like bottom	पजामी (*m.*)
business suit	सूट (*m.*)
slacks	पैंट (*f.*), पतलून (*f.*)
shirt	कमीज़ (*f.*)
pocket	जेब (*f.*)
tie	टाई (*f.*)
raincoat	बरसाती कोट (*m.*)
wraparound for men (one like Gandhi wore)	लाचा (*m.*), लुँगी (*f.*)
shorts	निक्कर (*f.*)
turban	पगड़ी (*f.*)
hat	टोप (*m.*)
cap	टोपी (*f.*)
handkerchief	रूमाल (*m.*)
wallet	बटुआ (*m.*)
socks	मोज़े (*m. pl.*), जुराबें (*f. pl.*)
shoes	जूते (*m. pl.*)

Jewelry • आभूषण, ज़ेवर

ring	अँगूठी (*f.*)
anklet	पायल (*f.*)
bracelet	कड़ा (*m.*)
bangles	चूड़ियाँ (*f. pl.*)
necklace	हार (*m.*), माला (*f.*)
dangling earrings (including chandelier)	झुमके (*m. pl.*)

studs	टॉप्स (*m.*)
general earrings	बुंदे (*m. pl.*)
nose ring	नथ (*f.*)
pendant for the forehead	टीका (*m.*)
pendant	लॉकेट (*m.*)

अभ्यास
२५·१

Circle the odd one out.

१. कमीज़, अचकन, चप्पल, कुर्ता

२. पेटीकोट, पजामा, पजामी, नथ

३. पेटी, स्वैटर, कोट, शॉल

४. गुलूबंद, चश्मा, हार, माला

५. चप्पल, जूते, गाउन, सैंडल

६. दस्ताने, दुपट्टा, अँगूठी, चूड़ियाँ

७. पगड़ी, टोप, घघरा, टोपी

८. घघरा, स्कर्ट, लुँगी, जेब

९. निक्कर, पैंट, बुंदे, जींस

१०. टॉप्स, झुमके, लॉकेट, बुंदे

अभ्यास
२५·२

ठीक या ग़लत *(True or false?)*

१. भारतीय औरतें सूट और साड़ी डालती हैं। _____

२. सर्दी में लोग कोट, स्वैटर, या शाल का इस्तेमाल करते हैं। _____

३. शहरों में कुछ लड़कियाँ जींस पहनती हैं। _____

४. लोग हाथों में चप्पल, सैंडल, या जूते पहनते हैं। _____

५. भारतीय आदमी हर रोज़ अचकन पहनते हैं। _____

६. बरसात में बरसाती कोट नहीं डालते। _____

७. लोग उँगली में अँगूठी और कलाई पर कड़ा या चूड़ी पहनते हैं। _____

८. औरतें और लड़कियाँ गले में हार, माला, या लॉकेट पहनती हैं। _____

९. लोग कमर पर टोप, टोपी, या पगड़ी पहनते हैं। _____

१०. पैसा पर्स, बटुआ, या जेब में रखते हैं। _____

The future tense • भविष्यकाल

The future tense is fairly straightforward. There are four suffixes that are added to the verb stem:

मैं	—ऊँगा/ऊँगी
तुम	—ओगे/ओगी
यह/वह/तू	—एगा/एगी
आप/हम/ये/वे	—एँगे/एँगी

Here is an example with the verb आना:

I will come	मैं आऊँगा। (*m. s.*)
I will come	मैं आऊँगी। (*f. s.*)
you (informal) *will come*	तू आएगा। (*m. s.*)
you (informal) *will come*	तू आएगी। (*f. s.*)
you (informal) *will come*	तुम आओगे। (*m. s.*)
you (informal) *will come*	तुम आओगी। (*f. s.*)
you (formal) *will come*	आप आएँगे। (*m. pl.*)
you (formal) *will come*	आप आएँगी। (*f. pl.*)
he/it will come	यह, वह आएगा। (*m. s.*)
she/it will come	यह, वह आएगी। (*f. s.*)
we will come	हम आएँगे। (*m. pl.*)
we will come	हम आएँगी। (*f. pl.*)
they/these/those will come	ये, वे आएँगे। (*m. pl.*)
they/these/those will come	ये, वे आएँगी। (*f. pl.*)

अभ्यास
२५·३

Conjugate the verbs जाना *and* चलना *in the future tense.*

	<u>जाना</u>	<u>चलना</u>
मैं (*m.*)	_____	_____
मैं (*f.*)	_____	_____
तू/यह/वह (*m.*)	_____	_____
तू/यह/वह (*f.*)	_____	_____
तुम (*m.*)	_____	_____
तुम (*f.*)	_____	_____
आप/हम/ये/वे (*m.*)	_____	_____
आप/हम/ये/वे (*f.*)	_____	_____

हिंदी में लिखिए *(Write in Hindi.)*

१. Neelam (*f.*) will climb the mountain. _____

२. Will you (*formal*) work on Monday? _____

३. We will not wear this. _____

४. They will buy a new house. _____

५. She will knit the sweater. _____

Irregular verbs

In the future tense, verbs होना, लेना, और देना are conjugated a little differently from the rest, but follow the same pattern among themselves.

	होना	लेना	देना
मैं (*m.*)	हूँगा	लूँगा	दूँगा
मैं (*f.*)	हूँगी	लूँगी	दूँगी
तू/यह/वह (*m.*)	होगा	लेगा	देगा
तू/यह/वह (*f.*)	होगी	लेगी	देगी
तुम (*m.*)	होगे	लोगे	दोगे
तुम (*f.*)	होगी	लोगी	दोगी
आप/हम/ये/वे (*m.*)	होंगे	लेंगे	देंगे
आप/हम/ये/वे (*f.*)	होंगी	लेंगी	देंगी

हिंदी में लिखिए *(Write in Hindi.)*

१. I (*female*) will be in the garden. _____

२. We will take matar paneer. _____

३. What will you (*informal*) give her on her birthday? _____

४. Where will they be at that time? _____

५. Who will give the money? _____

६. When will it be Christmas? (क्रिसमस, बड़ा दिन) _____

Some more useful verbs

to break	तोड़ना
to put together	जोड़ना
to lose	खोना
to find, receive	को मिलना (मिलना has other meanings too)
to spend	खर्चना
to save	बचाना
to stand	खड़ा होना
to worry	चिंता करना
to suggest	सुझाव देना
to donate	दान करना

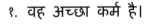

अभ्यास
२५·६

हिंदी में लिखिए *(Write in Hindi.)*

१. I will not spend a lot. _____

२. She is worrying. _____

३. He was saving. _____

४. They will donate clothes. _____

५. What will we receive? _____

Reading practice • पढ़ने का अभ्यास

For added practice and information, underline the Hindi words that have made their way into English in these sentences and provide the English equivalent.

१. वह अच्छा कर्म है। _____

२. वे कल योग करेंगे। _____

३. पंडित जी/गुरु जी से मिलिए। _____

४. मुझे कश्मीरी स्वैटर पसंद हैं। _____

५. उसे खाकी रंग पसंद है। _____

६. आज हम बंगले में जाएँगे। _____

७. वह दुकान लूट रहा था। _____

८. निर्वाण का मतलब क्या है? _____

Answer key
कुँजी

 **THE HINDI ALPHABET**

1 Vowels

1·1 1. इ i   2. ऊ ū   3. अ a   4. औ au   5. ऋ r̩   6. ई ī   7. ए e
8. ओ o   9. आ ā   10. अं m̩   11. उ u   12. ऐ ai   13. अः ḥ

1·2

SHORT	LONG	SHORT	LONG	SHORT	LONG
अ	आ	इ	ई	उ	ऊ
ऋ	ए	ऐ	ओ	औ	
	अं			अः	

2 Consonants

2·1 1. D   2. A   3. A   4. B   5. C   6. B   7. B   8. D   9. C   10. D

3 Writing consonants

3·1 1. क k   2. ख kh   3. ग g   4. घ gh   5. च c
6. छ ch   7. ज j   8. झ jh   9. ट ṭ

3·2 1. ठ ṭh   2. ड ḍ   3. ढ ḍh   4. ण ṇ   5. त t
6. थ th   7. द d   8. ध dh   9. न n

4 Writing more consonants

4·1 1. ब b   2. भ bh   3. म m   4. य y   5. र r
6. ल l   7. व v   8. श ś   9. ष ṣ   10. ह h   11. ड़ ṛ

4·2 1. ढ़ ṛh   2. क़ k̩   3. ख़ k̩h   4. ग़ ġ   5. ज़ z
6. फ़ f   7. क्ष kṣ   8. त्र tr   9. ज्ञ jñ   10. श्र śra

4·3 1. फ   2. य   3. र   4. श   5. स   6. ड   7. त्र

4·4 1. gh vs. dh   2. c vs. y vs. th   3. j vs. c   4. g vs. m vs. bh   5. i vs. ī vs. jh
6. ṭ vs. ṭh   7. ḍ vs. i   8. dh vs. d   9. v vs. b   10. r vs. ś
11. p vs. ṣ   12. kh vs. r vs. v   13. a vs. u   14. ā vs. o

4·5 No key required.

4·6 No key required.

Reading practice

Nouns: आम—ām, घर—ghar, छत—chat, जल—jal, नल—nal, ऊन—ūn, श्रम—śram, बस—bas, हक़—haḳ.
Verbs: पढ़—paṛh, कर—kar, चल—cal, रख—rakh, हट—haṭ, चख—cakh, ढल—ḍhal, थक—thak, फ़ट—faṭ, ढक—ḍhak

II HINDI WORDS

5 Diacritic marks

5·1 1. ग (ga)   2. गा (gā)   3. गि (gi)   4. गी (gī)   5. गु (gu)   6. गू (gū)   7. गृ (gṛ)
      8. गे (ge)   9. गै (gai)   10. गो (go)   11. गौ (gau)   12. गं (gṃ)   13. गँ (gṃ)   14. गः (gḥ)

5·2 1. घ (gha)   2. घा (ghā)   3. घि (ghi)   4. घी (ghī)   5. घु (ghu)   6. घू (ghū)
      7. घृ (ghṛ)   8. घे (ghe)   9. घै (ghai)   10. घो (gho)   11. घौ (ghau)   12. घं (ghṃ)
      13. घँ (ghṃ)   14. घः (ghḥ)

5·3 1. द (da)   2. दा (dā)   3. दि (di)   4. दी (dī)   5. दु (du)   6. दू (dū)   7. दृ (dṛ)
      8. दे (de)   9. दै (dai)   10. दो (do)   11. दौ (dau)   12. दं (dṃ)   13. दँ (dṃ)   14. दः (dḥ)

5·4 1. Cī, chai, chu   2. ṭhu, ṭhū, ḍhī   3. thi, bhi, bhau   4. lu, ru, rū   5. śī, hu, hṛ   6. kṣu, śr, sa

5·5 1. अ – धन (dhan = wealth)   2. आ – लाभ (lābh = benefit)   3. इ – फिर (fir = again)
      4. ई – वीर (vīr = brave)   5. उ – शुभ (śubh = opportune)   6. ऊ – नूर (nūr = light)
      7. ऋ – गृह (gṛeh = house)   8. ए – देश (deś = country)   9. ऐ – सैर (sair = stroll)
      10. ओ – रोज़ (roz = everyday)   11. औ – शौक़ (śauk = hobby)   12. अं – रंग (raṃg = color)
      13. अँ – मुँह (muṃh = mouth)   14. अः – अतः (ataḥ = therefore)

5·6 1. कपड़े (kapaṛe)   2. दो मेज़ (do mez)   3. क़लम (ḳalam)   4. कुछ काग़ज़ (kuch kāġaz)
      5. किताब (kitāb)   6. जूते (jute)   7. चाबी (cābī)   8. एक लैपटाप (ek laiptop)
      9. पानी की बोतल (pānī kī botal)   10. गिलास (gilās)

6 Conjunct characters I

6·1 1. राज्य   2. स्थल   3. रफ़्तार   4. शुल्क   5. अन्य   6. मध्य
      7. सूक्ष्म   8. लम्बा   9. चश्मा   10. मुख्य

7 Conjunct characters II and III

7·1 1. शब्द   2. अच्छा   3. धन्यवाद   4. अर्थ   5. क्या
      6. हिन्दुस्तान   7. कृप्या   8. शुक्रिया   9. रास्ता   10. उम्र

7·2 1. हिन्दी   2. दिल्ली   3. राज्य   4. प्रश्न   5. उत्तर
      6. शुद्ध   7. शक्ति   8. मुक्ति   9. द्वार   10. विद्यालय

7·3 1. पत्र   2. किताब   3. मेज़   4. घंटा   5. दिन
      6. कक्षा   7. सुबह   8. सामान   9. वक़्त   10. अच्छा

7·4 1. नमस्ते, मेरा नाम _____ है।

      2. आपका नाम क्या है or आपका क्या नाम है?

      3. आप से मिलकर खुशी हुई।

      4. आप कैसे हैं?

      5. मैं अच्छा/अच्छी हूँ (for male/female speakers, respectively), धन्यवाद or शुक्रिया।

      6. फिर मिलेंगे।

Reading practice

1. False   2. False   3. False   4. True   5. True

III HINDI SENTENCES

8 Sentence structure

8·1 1. German जर्मन 2. Vietnamese वियतनामी 3. English अँग्रेज़/ब्रितानी
4. Greek यूनानी 5. French फ्रांसीसी 6. Indian हिन्दुस्तानी/भारतीय
7. Bhutanese भूटानी 8. Australian ऑस्ट्रेलियन 9. Iraqi ईराकी
10. Iranian ईरानी

8·2 1. सूकी जापानी है। 2. डेविड इज़राइली है। 3. सोनिया अमरीकी है।
4. पेमा नेपाली है। 5. चाओ चीनी है। 6. ओलिविय फ्रांसीसी है।
7. हमीद अफ़ग़ानी है। 8. नीलोफ़र पाकिस्तानी है। 9. शहनाज़ बंगलादेशी/बंगला है।
10. माईकल ब्रितानी है। 11. मारियो इतालवी है। 12. व्लैडिमिर रूसी है।
13. सोफ़ी अफ़्रीकी है। 14. किरन ऐशियाई है।

8·3 1. हम 2. तू, तुम 3. मैं 4. आप 5. यह 6. वह 7. य 8. वे

8·4 1. मैं हूँ 2. तू है 3. तुम हो 4. आप हैं 5. यह/वह है 6. ये/वे हैं 7. हम हैं

8·5 1. मैं हूँ 2. यह/वह है 3. यह/वह है 4. ये/वे हैं 5. वे हैं 6. हम हैं 7. तू है/तुम हो 8. आप हैं

8·6 1. thief चोर 2. jeweler जौहरी 3. sculptor मूर्तीकार
4. mechanic मिस्त्री 5. tourist पर्यटक 6. musician संगीतकार
7. hairdresser नाई 8. confectioner हलवाई 9. dancer नर्तक, नर्तकी
10. carpenter बढ़ई

8·7 1. मैं राजनायक हूँ। 2. यह/वह अध्यापिका है। 3. यह/वह किसान है।
4. ये/वे वकील हैं। 5. वे वकील हैं। 6. हम चालक हैं।
7. तुम डाकिया हो। 8. आप दर्ज़ी हैं।

9 Questions and answers

9·1 1. पुलिस वाला 2. पैसे वाला
3. बस वाला 4. खिलौने वाला
5. टैक्सी वाला

9·2 1. क्या आप एक कलाकार हैं? 2. जी हाँ, मैं एक कलाकार हूँ।
3. क्या वह आदमी भारतीय है? 4. जी हाँ, वह भारतीय है।
5. क्या वह औरत एक अभियंता है? 6. जी नहीं, वह अभियंता नहीं है।
7. क्या वे लोग व्यापारी हैं? 8. जी नहीं, वे व्यापारी नहीं, राजनायक हैं।
9. क्या ये चीज़ें बंगलादेशी हैं? 10. जी नहीं, वे बंगलादेशी नहीं, पाकिस्तानी हैं।

9·3 1. और 2. लेकिन/पर/मगर 3. दोनों 4. दोनों 5. और 6. लेकिन/पर/मगर

Reading practice

1. Transliteration: Amitābh Baccan bhārat kā ek prasidh abhinetā hai.
Amitabh Bacchan is a famous actor of India.

2. Transliteration: Mahātmā Gāñdhī kā nām Mohandās Karamcañd Gāñdhī thā.
Mahatma Gandhi's name was Mohandas Karamchand Gandhi.

3. Transliteration: Sabīr Bhātiā hotmel kā sañsthāpak hai.
Sabeer Bhatia is the founder of Hotmail.

4. Transliteration: Madhur Jāfrī kī kaī kitābeñ haiñ.
Madhur Jaffrey has several books.

5. Transliteration: Madar ṭarīsā kalkattā maiñ kām kartī thīñ.
Mother Teresa used to work in Calcutta.

6. Transliteration: Gāyikā Norāh Joñs ādhī bhārtiya hai.
   Singer Norah Jones is half Indian.

7. Transliteration: Bobī Jindal Luīsiānā, Amrīkā kā pahlā bhārtiya-amrīkī rājyapāl hai.
   Bobby Jindal is Louisiana, America's first Indian–American governor.

8. Transliteration: Sunītā Wiliams añtarikṣ maiñ sabse lambī yātrā karnevālī pahlī aurat hai.
   Sunita Williams is the first woman to make the longest journey in space.

9. Transliteration: Mīrā Neyar aur M. Nāīt śyāmālan dono dilcasp filmaiñ banāte haiñ.
   Mira Nair and M. Night Shyamalan both make interesting films.

10. Transliteration: Latā Mañgeśkar bhārat kī ek prasidh gāyīkā haiñ.
    Lata Mangeshkar is one of India's famous singers.

True/False: 1. F   2. F   3. T   4. F   5. T

◆IV◆ THE PRESENT TENSE

10 The present indefinite

10·1
1. आना—to come
2. जाना—to go
3. जागना—to awake
4. खाना—to eat
5. पीना—to drink
6. सोना—to sleep
7. नहाना—to bathe, shower
8. पढ़ना—to read, study
9. लिखना—to write
10. करना—to do
11. देखना—to see, watch
12. चलाना—to drive (something)

10·2
1. (m. s.): मैं <u>आता</u> हूँ।
2. (f. s.): मैं <u>आती</u> हूँ।
3. (m. s.): तू <u>आता</u> है।
4. (f. s.): तू <u>आती</u> है।
5. (m. s.): तुम <u>आते</u> हो।
6. (f. s.): तुम <u>आती</u> हो।
7. (m. pl.): आप <u>आते</u> हैं।
8. (f. pl.): आप <u>आती</u> हैं।
9. (m. pl.): हम <u>आते</u> हैं।
10. (f. pl.): हम <u>आती</u> हैं।
11. (m. s.): यह/वह <u>आता</u> है।
12. (f. s.): यह/वह <u>आती</u> है।
13. (m. pl.): ये/वे <u>आते</u> हैं।
14. (f. pl.): ये/वे <u>आती</u> हैं।

10·3
1. Correct
2. Correct
3. Correct
4. Correct
5. Incorrect
6. Correct
7. Incorrect
8. Incorrect
9. Incorrect
10. Incorrect
11. Correct
12. Correct
13. Incorrect
14. Correct

10·4
1. मैं खाता और पीता हूँ।
2. यह/वह जागती है।
3. ये/वे नहाते हैं।
4. आप टी.वी. देखते हैं।
5. तुम लिखती हो।
6. वे जीतते हैं।
7. हम चलते हैं।
8. यह/वह उड़ता है।

10·5 Answers may vary.

11 Numbers

११·१
१. 522-423765989
२. 22-213664708
३. आपका पता क्या है?

११·२
१. आपका फ़ोन नम्बर क्या है?
२. मेरा फ़ोन नम्बर 11-423765989 है।
३. आज क्या तारीख़ है?
४. आज की तारीख़ उन्नीस जून है।
५. आप कितने साल के हैं?
६. मैं उनतीस साल का हूँ।
७. आपकी उम्र/आयु क्या है?
८. मेरी उम्र/आयु बाईस साल है।
९. मैं चौबीस वर्ष की हूँ।

११·३ Answers may vary.

12 Possessives

12·1
1. our/ours हमारा hamārā (*m. s.*), हमारी hamārī (*f.*), हमारे hamāre (*m. pl.*)
2. your/yours (*informal*) तू: तेरा terā (*m. s.*), तेरी terī (*f.*), तेरे tere (*m. pl.*)
3. your/yours (*informal*) तुम्हारा tumhārā (*m. s.*), तुम्हारी tumhārī (*f.*), तुम्हारे tumhāre (*m. pl.*)
4. their/theirs (proximity) इनका inkā (*m. s.*), इनकी inkī (*f.*), इनके inke (*m. pl.*)
5. my/mine मेरा merā (*m. s.*), मेरी merī (*f.*), मेरे mere (*m. pl.*)
6. his/her/its (proximity) इसका iskā (*m. s.*), इसकी iskī (*f.*), इसके iske (*m. pl.*)
7. your/yours (*formal*) आपका āpkā (*m. s.*), आपकी āpkī (*f.*), आपके āpke (*m. pl.*)
8. his/her/its (distance) उसका uskā (*m. s.*), उसकी uskī (*f.*), उसके uske (*m. pl.*)
9. their/theirs (distance) उनका unkā (*m. s.*), उनकी unkī (*f.*), उनके unke (*m. pl.*)

12·2
1. आपके काग़ज़
2. इसकी/उसकी पानी की बोतल
3. तेरी चाबी
4. इनके/उनके कपड़े
5. इसके/उसके जूते
6. इसके/उसके जूते
7. तेरी/तुम्हारी क़लम
8. इनका/उनका गिलास
9. हमारा मेज़
10. आपकी किताब

12·3
1. यह मेरा मेज़ है।
2. यह आपकी चाबी है।
3. यह तुम्हारा लैपटाप है।
4. यह तेरा गिलास है।
5. यह हमारी पानी की बोतल है।
6. यह इसका/उसका मेज़ है।
7. यह इनकी/उनकी चाबी है।

12·4
1. उनकी किताब यूनानी है।
2. हमारा मेज़ भारतीय है।
3. वे आपकी किताब पढ़ते हैं।
4. वह इसकी/उसकी चाबी नहीं, आपकी है।
5. क्या वे मेरे जूते हैं?
6. नहीं, वे तुम्हारे नहीं, इसके/उसके हैं।
7. क्या यह लैपटाप तुम्हारा है?
8. हाँ, यह लैपटाप मेरा है, पर वह लैपटाप तुम्हारा है।
9. ये पाँच गिलास मेरे हैं।
10. वह क़लम इसकी/उसकी है।
11. ये कपड़े हमारे हैं।
12. मैं तेरी गाड़ी चलाती हूँ।

Reading practice

Rājeś kī dincaryā

Transliteration: Rājeś subah jaldī uṭhtā hai. Vah nahātā hai aur dānt sāf karta hai. Fir, vah nāśtā banātā hai aur khātā hai. Vah kapṛe pahantā hai aur daftar jātā hai. Vahāñ kām kartā hai. Dopahar ko khānā khātā hai. śām ko kharidārī kartā hai aur ghar ātā hai. Vah saṅgīt suntā hai aur patrikā paṛhtā hai. Vah rāt kā khānā khātā hai aur fir sotā hai.

English translation: Rajesh gets up early in the morning. He showers and brushes his teeth. Then, he makes breakfast and eats. He wears clothes and goes to the office. Over there, he works. In the afternoon, he eats. In the evening, he shops and comes home. He listens to music and reads a magazine. He has dinner and then sleeps.

Yes/No: 1. जी नहीं   2. जी नहीं   3. जी नहीं   4. जी हाँ   5. जी नहीं

V NOUNS

13 People

13·1
1. पति, पत्नी
2. पिता, माता
3. बेटा/पुत्र, बेटी/पुत्री
4. भाई/भैया, बहन/बहिन
5. बड़ा/छोटा भाई, बड़ी/छोटी बहन
6. नाना, नानी
7. दादा, दादी
8. ससुर, सास
9. मामा, मामी
10. मौसा, मौसी
11. चाचा, चाची

१३·२	१. पिता जी	२. माता जी	३. बड़ा भाई
	४. छोटा भाई	५. बड़ी बहन	६. छोटी बहन
१३·३	१. पति	२. बेटा	३. बेटी
	४. नाना	५. नानी	
१३·४	१. रविवार	२. सोमवार	३. मंगलवार और बुधवार
	४. गुरुवार	५. शुक्रवार और शनिवार	

१३·५ १. मेरा जन्मदिन दिसम्बर में होता है। २. मेरी बहन का जन्मदिन फ़रवरी में होता है।

३. आज की तारीख २ मई है।

14 Places

१४·१	१. विश्वविद्यालय जाती है	२. अस्पताल में काम करती है
	३. डाकघर जाती है	४. सिनेमाघर जाती है
	५. घर रहती है	५. रेस्तरां में खाती है
	७. गिरजाघर में पूजा करती है	

१४·२	१. विद्यार्थी, छात्रावास	२. अध्यापक, विद्यालय
	३. बावरची (cook/chef), भोजनालय	४. चिकित्सक, चिकित्सालय
	५. माली, बाग	६. शेर (lion), चिड़ियाघर
	७. विक्रेता, बाज़ार	८. हवाई जहाज़ (airplane), हवाई अड्डा
	९. डाकिया, डाकघर	१०. खज़ाँची, बैंक
	११. ईसाई (Christian), गिरजाघर	१२. हिंदु (Hindu), मंदिर
	१३. सिख (Sikh), गुरुद्वारा	१४. मुसलमान (Muslim), मस्जिद

१४·३	१. हम जापान से हैं।	२. पर, वे चीन से हैं।	३. दोनों भारत से हैं।
	४. आप यूनान से हैं।	५. तुम अफ़्रीका से हो।	६. फ़्रैंक यूरोप से है।
	७. राधा कैनेडा से है।		

१४·४ Answers may vary.

१४·५	१. से प्यार करते हैं	२. से शादी करती हो	३. से लड़ते हैं
	४. से हाथ मिलाते हैं	५. से नाराज़ होता/होती हूँ	६. से डरता है
	७. से पूछता/पूछती है	८. से बात करता/करती है	

१४·६ १. Correct २. Incorrect ३. Incorrect ४. Correct ५. Incorrect

१४·७	१. में	२. को	३. में	४. पर	५. में	६. से	७. से	८. पर	९. तक
	१०. में	११. में	१२. को						

15 Around the house

१५·१	१. संग्रहालय	२. बैंक	३. लेखक	४. घर
	५. पिता	६. अभिनेता	७. अभियंता	८. विक्रेता
	९. बेटे	१०. बस अड्डे	११. बगीचे	१२. पोते
	१३. पति	१४. भाई	१५. दर्जी	१६. ताऊ
१५·२	१. क़लमें	२. बहनें	३. क़िताबें	४. रातें
	५. माताएँ	६. गायिकाएँ	७. बुआएँ	८. लेखिकाएँ
	९. चाबियाँ	१०. बेटियाँ	११. अभिनेत्रियाँ	१२. चिड़ियाँ
	१३. गुड़ियाँ	१४. बिटियाँ		
१५·३	१. गिरजाघर	२. बिटियाँ	३. अभियंता	४. काग़ज़
	५. चाचियाँ	६. बहुएँ	७. हवाई अड्डे	८. माताएँ
	९. खज़ाँची			

१५·४	१. दरवाज़े	२. घंटियाँ	३. पायदान	४. सीढ़ियाँ
	५. खिड़कियाँ	६. कालीन	७. दरियाँ	८. पंखे
	९. दीवारें	१०. तस्वीरें	११. चित्र	१२. अलमारियाँ
	१३. कुर्सियाँ	१४. टी. वी	१५. छुरियाँ	१६. कांटे
	१७. चम्मच	१८. गिलास	१९. थालियाँ	२०. पलंग
	२१. बिस्तर	२२. तकिए	२३. रजाइयाँ	२४. कंबल
	२५. चादरें	२६. पर्दे	२७. शीशे	२८. नल
	२९. साबुन	३०. तौलिए	३१. पेड़	३२. पौधे
	३३. झाड़ियाँ	३४. फूल	३५. फव्वारे	३६. गमले

१५·५ Answers vary.

१५·६ There are several correct responses. The chart below presents one possible placement of items. Some items can be placed in more than one part of the house.

बैठक	रसोई	शयन कक्ष	स्नानघर	बगीचा	गैराज
चित्र	छुरी	कंबल	शीशा	झाड़ी	झाड़ू
कालीन	कूड़ेदान	तकिया	साबुन	गमला	पोछा
मेज़	थाली	तौलिया	नल	फूल	गाड़ी
लैंप	कांटा	गद्दा	टूथब्रश	फव्वारा	
पर्दा	प्लेट	पलंग	टूथपेस्ट	पौधा	
सोफ़ा	बर्तन	बिस्तर	आईना	पेड़	
फूलदान	अलमारी	चादर		पत्ता	
टी. वी.	गिलास	रजाई			

16   More verbs and possessives

१६·१ Some answers may vary.

	१. जोसफ़ पंखा चलाता है।	२. हम रसोई में खाना पकाते हैं।
	३. वे दोनों दरवाज़ा खोलते हैं।	४. आप घंटी बजाते हैं।
	५. साहिल कूड़ा फैंकता है।	६. यह पायदान पर जूते साफ़ करता है।
	७. रोहित फ़र्श पर चलता है।	८. शोभा दीवार पर तस्वीरें टाँगती है।
	९. क्या तुम फूलदान में फूल डालते हो?	१०. पिता जी कुर्सी पर बैठते हैं।
	११. माता जी लैंप जलाती हैं।	१२. छोटी बहन दरी बिछाती है।
	१३. बड़ा भाई झाड़ू लगाता है।	१४. नानी जी रजाई ओढ़ती हैं।
	१५. नवीन बाग में घूमता है।	

१६·२

	१. डैन का टी.वी.	२. कारला का पंखा	३. बाब की दरी
	४. ईयन के जूते	५. समैंथा का घर	६. ऐल के पिता जी
	७. गैविन की माता जी	८. हैरी की बहन	९. सबरीना का भाई
	१०. क्रिस की गाड़ी		

Reading practice

Translation:

Republic Day is celebrated on January 26th.

Holi is celebrated in March.

Baisakhi is on April 13th.

The festival of Raksha Bandhan/Rakhi is in August.

Independence Day is celebrated on August 15th.

Vijaydashmi/Dusshera is in October.

Karva Chauth is in October.

Deepavali/Diwali is in October or November.

Name the festival:

१. होली

२. दीपावली/दीवाली

३. स्वतंत्रता दिवस

४. करवा चौथ

५. बैसाखी

६. गणतंत्र दिवस

७. रक्षा बंधन/राखी

८. विजयदशमी/दशहरा

◆VI ADJECTIVES

17 Describing things

१७·१ १. हरे पौधे
२. बैंगनी फूल
३. भूरे पेड़
४. रंग-बिरंगा फ़व्वारा
५. गुलाबी चादर
६. सफ़ेद तकिए
७. लाल दरी
८. सुनहरा सोफ़ा
९. नीले दरवाज़े
१०. संतरी तस्वीरें

१७·२ १. वह डाक घर किस रंग का है?
२. वह स्लेटी है।
३. ये लाल कुर्सियाँ किसकी हैं?
४. ये पैट्रिक की हैं।
५. पत्ते किस रंग के होते हैं?
६. वे हरे होते हैं।
७. वह चादर किस रंग की है?
८. वह हरी है।

१७·३ १. ग़लत   २. ठीक   ३. ग़लत   ४. ठीक   ६. ग़लत

१७·४ १. छोटी   २. मोटा   ३. अच्छे   ४. ख़ूबसूरत   ५. चौड़ी   ६. गर्म   7. लंबे   ८. हल्के

९. खुल   १०. खुश   ११. मँहगा   १२. ख़ास   १३. अमीर   १४. आम   १५. पुरानी

18 Comparisons

१८·१ Answers may vary.

१. सूपरमैन अच्छा और ताकतवर आदमी है।

२. बग्ज़ बन्नी तेज़ और चालाक खरगोश है।

३. दिसम्बर में दिल्ली का मौसम ठंडा होता है।

४. वाइट हाउस एक सफ़ेद और ख़ूबसूरत इमारत है।

५. हिमालय ऊँचा और बड़ा है।

१८·२ १. जून में अमरीका का मौसम कैसा होता है?

२. आपका बगीचा कैसा है?

३. यह प्रश्न कैसा है?

४. आपका कुत्ता कैसा है?

५. यह बात कैसी है?

१८·३ १. सबसे   २. से, से ज़्यादा   ३. से कम   ४. से ज़्यादा   ५. सबसे ज़्यादा

१८·४ १. यह टी.वी. उस टी.वी. से ज़्यादा महँगा है।

२. उस घर से यह घर बेहतर है।

३. मुझ से माता जी प्रश्न पूछते हैं।

४. तुम वह से डरता है।

५. मेरा लैपटाप उन के लैपटाप से कम भारी है।

१८·५   १. यह संग्रहालय उस संग्रहालय से बड़ा है।   २. हम पंखा इस मेज़ पर रखते हैं।

३. आप उन से बात करते हैं।   ४. वे तुम से बात करते हैं।

५. तुम मुझ से हाथ मिलाते हो।

१८·६   १. मुझे किताबें पढ़ना पसंद है।   २. मुझे सुबह उठना पसंद नहीं।

३. रात को उसे, इसे सोना चाहिए।   ४. उन्हें नया घर चाहिए।

५. उसे, इसे सृजन अच्छी लगती है।   ६. रीमा को सोमवार को काम करना अच्छा नहीं लगता।

19   Food and drink

१९·१   १. गोभी   २. दूध   ३. मटन   ४. पानी   ५. दही   ६. चाय   ७. केंकड़ा   ८. नारियल   ९. पनीर   १०. खीर

१९·२   Answers vary.

१९·३   Answers may vary.

१. गुलाब जामुनः नर्म   २. गाजरः सख्त   ३. पकोड़ाः नमकीन

४. लीचीः मीठी   ५. हलवाः मीठा   ६. इमलीः खट्टी

७. पापड़ः मसालेदार   ८. चटनीः खट्टी-मीठी   ९. ताज़ा पुदीनाः कड़वा

१०. कल की लस्सीः बासी

१९·४   १. पानी—तैरना, गोताखोरी   २. टी.वी.—टी.वी. देखना   ३. गाड़ी—गाड़ी में घूमना

४. बास्केट—बास्केटबाल   ५. दो लोग—कुश्ती   ६. मुक्का—मुक्केबाज़ी

७. साईकल—साईकल चलाना   ८. बाग—बागबानी करना   ९. कैमरा—फोटो खींचना

१०. मछली—मछली पकड़ना

१९·५   २. X   ४. X   ५. X   ६. X   ७. X   ८. X

१९·६   Answers vary.

Reading practice

Complete the idiom:

१. कीमा   २. खिचड़ी   ३. मुर्गी   ४. घी   ५. पानी का पानी

६. नमक   ७. मक्खन   ८. काला   ९. खीर   १०. पानी

VII   POSTPOSITIONS AND THE PAST TENSE

20   Postpositions

२०·१   १. छोटे घर में   २. छोटे घरों में   ३. बड़ी दरी पर

४. बड़ी दरियों पर   ५. ख़ूबसूरत औरत को   ६. ख़ूबसूरत औरतों को

७. पतले आदमी से   ८. पतले आदमियों से   ९. ऊँचे पहाड़ का

१०. ऊँचे पहाड़ों का   ११. पीली कुर्सी तक   १२. पीली कुर्सियों तक

२०·२   १. उस छोटे घर में   २. उन छोटे घरों में   ३. उस/इस की बड़ी दरी पर

४. उस/इस की बड़ी दरियों पर   ५. उस ख़ूबसूरत औरत को   ६. उन ख़ूबसूरत औरतों को

७. इस पतले आदमी से   ८. इन पतले आदमियों से   ९. उस ऊँचे पहाड़ का

१०. उन ऊँचे पहाड़ों का   ११. इस/उस की पीली कुर्सी तक   १२. इस/उस की पीली कुर्सियों तक

२०·३   १. बेटे से, बेटों से   २. हवाई अड्डे में, हवाई अड्डों में   ३. पिता का, पिताओं का

४. कद्दू पर, कद्दुओं पर   ५. बेटी से, बेटियों से   ६. माँ/माता को, माँओं/माताओं को

७. बहन का, बहनों का   ८. गुड़िया पर, गुड़ियों पर

२०·४ १. उस अच्छे बेटे से, उन अच्छे बेटों से

२. इस बड़े हवाई अड्डे में, इन बड़े हवाई अड्डों में

३. इस बूढ़े पिता का, इन बूढ़े पिताओं का

४. इस सुनहरे कद्दू पर, इन सुनहरे कद्दुओं पर

५. उस ख़ूबसूरत बेटी से, उन ख़ूबसूरत बेटियों से

६. मेरी अच्छी माँ/माता को, मेरी अच्छी माँओं/माताओं को

७. इस/उस की छोटी बहन का, इस/उस की छोटी बहनों का

८. इस/उस की मँहगी गुड़िया पर, इस/उस की मँहगी गुड़ियों पर

२०·५ १. ये भूरी अलमारियाँ मेरी पुरानी रसोई में हैं। २. यह ख़ूबसूरत फूल इस मँहगे फूलदान में है।

३. क्या वे केले उस छोटे बगीचे से हैं? ४. ये ख़ूबसूरत पर्दे उन चौड़ी खिड़कियों पर हैं।

५. रंग-बिरंगी तस्वीरें उन फ्रांसीसी दरवाज़ों पर हैं।

२०·६ १. Correct २. Incorrect ३. Correct ४. Correct ५. Incorrect ६. Correct

७. Correct ८. Correct ९. Correct १०. Incorrect

२०·७ १. इस/उस के पुराने गैराज में २. मेरी बहन के जन्मदिन पर ३. आज की तारीख स

४. आपके घर तक ५. तुम्हारे पिता को

२०·८ १. आपकी कितनी बहनें हैं? २. मेरी एक बहन है। ३. तुम्हारी कितनी गाड़ियाँ हैं?

४. ये सेब कितने के हैं? ५. नाशपाति कितनी मँहगी है! ६. यह इमारत कितनी ख़ूबसूरत है!

७. प्याज़ कितने के हैं? ८. गाजरें कितने की हैं?

21 Animals and the senses

२१·१ Some answers may vary.

१. केंकड़ा, रेस्तरां में २. अजगर, चिड़िया घर में ३. कबूतर, छत पर

४. केंचुआ, ज़मीन पर ५. गिलहरी, बगीचे में ६. बिल्ली, घर में

७. चील, आसमान में ८. चूहा, पिंजरे में (in the cage) ९. मछली, पानी में

१०. शेर, जंगल में

२१·२ १. ठीक २. ठीक ३. ग़लत ४. ठीक ५. ग़लत ६. ठीक ७. ठीक ८. ग़लत ९. ठीक १०. ठीक

२१·३ १. छोटे काले बाल: short black hair २. ख़ूबसूरत चेहरा: beautiful face

३. बड़ा माथा: big forehead ४. लाल कनपट्टियाँ: red temples

५. गहरी भूरी आँखें: dark brown eyes ६. लंबी पलकें: long eyelashes

७. गुलाबी होंठ: pink lips ८. सफेद दाँत: white teeth

९. चौड़े कंधे: wide shoulders १०. पतली उँगलियाँ: long fingers

२१·४ १. ठीक २. ग़लत ३. ठीक ४. ठीक ५. ग़लत ६. ग़लत ७. ग़लत ८. ग़लत

२१·५ Answers vary

२१·६ १. इस/उस को खाँसी है। २. इस/उस को छींक आती है। ३. उन को खुजली होती है।

४. हमें ज़ुकाम है। ५. आप को बुख़ार है। ६. मुझे नज़ला है।

७. तुम्हें सूजन है।

२१·७ १. के आगे २. के सामने ३. के पीछे

४. के ऊपर ५. के नीचे ६. के बीच में

७. के दौरान ८. के बारे में ९. के आसपास

१०. के बाद

२१·८ Some answers may vary.

१. के आगे २. के ऊपर ३. के साथ ४. के नीचे ५. के सामने ६. की बगल में

७. के पास ८. के ऊपर ९. के पीछे १०. के सिवा

22 The past tense

२२·१ १. यह गाड़ी चलाइए।   २. कल मेरा काम करो/करना।

३. उस/इस से पूछो/पूछना।   ४. बत्ती जलाइए।

५. दरवाज़ा बंद कीजिए।   ६. खाना बनाओ/बनाना।

२२·२ १. गाड़ी धो।   २. कोशिश करो।

३. बस पकड़ो।   ४. तुम आराम करो।

५. आज काम शुरु कीजिए।   ६. कमरा साफ़ करो।

७. कल तक दिल्ली पहुँचिए।   ८. हर रोज़ हँसो।

९. दरवाज़ा खोलो।   १०. दरवाज़ा बंद कीजिए।

२२·३ १. सिर्फ़ २. भी ३. सिर्फ़ ४. मत ५. भी ६. मत

२२·४ १. What is the flight number? मेरा उड़ान नम्बर क्या है?

२. Where is the security check? सुरक्षा जाँच किधर है?

३. This is my luggage. यह मेरा सामान है।

४. This is not my luggage. यह मेरा सामान नहीं है।

५. I want to rent a car. मैं एक गाड़ी किराए पर लेना चाहता हूँ।

६. Go straight. सीधा चलो।

७. Turn right at the traffic light. लाल बत्ती पर बाएं मुड़ो।

८. Park here. यहाँ पर पार्क करो।

९. Stop here. यहाँ रुको।

१०. Is there a gas station nearby? क्या आसपास कोई पैट्रोल पम्प है?

११. Turn left at the intersection. चौराहे पर दाएं मुड़ो।

१२. Do you have insurance? आप के पास बीमा है?

१३. Is there a mechanic shop nearby? आसपास कोई मिस्त्री की दुकान है?

२२·५ १. क्या आप मेरी मदद कर सकते हैं?   २. मैं पहिया बदलना चाहता हूँ।

३. इस उड़ान का द्वार नम्बर क्या है?   ४. लीसा इन किधर है?

५. यह निकास ढलान लो।

२२·६ १. (*m. s.*): मैं आता था।   २. (*f. s.*): मैं आती थी।

३. (*m. s.*): तू आता था।   ४. (*f. s.*): तू आती थी।

५. (*m. s.*): तुम आते थे।   ६. (*f. s.*): तुम आती थीं।

७. (*m. pl.*): यह/वह आता था।   ८. (*f. pl.*): यह/वह आती थी।

९. (*m. pl.*): आप आते थे।   १०. (*f. pl.*): आप आती थीं।

११. (*m. s.*): हम आते थे।   १२. (*f. s.*): हम आती थीं।

१३. (*m. pl.*): ये/वे आते थे।   १४. (*f. pl.*): ये/वे आती थीं।

२२·७ १. मैं हर रोज़ टी. वी. देखती थी।   २. वह रविवार को आराम करती थी।

३. हम हँसते थे।   ४. वे हम से बात करते थे।

५. यह/वह सस्ता होता था।

Reading practice

Translation: How does one make Masala Chai?

१. Grind one clove, some cardamom seeds, a little cinnamon, and ginger.

२. Put all these things in a cup of water and boil.

३. Put a pinch of black pepper.

४. Put half cup milk and sugar to taste.

५. Mix a tablespoon of tea leaves and boil again.

६. Then, strain it in a cup or kettle and drink!

VIII THE CONTINUOUS AND FUTURE TENSES

23 Time

२३·१
१. चार बजे हैं।
२. सवा छः बजे हैं।
३. सवा आठ बजे हैं।
४. साढ़े तीन बजे हैं।
५. साढ़े पाँच बजे हैं।
६. डेढ़ बजे हैं।
७. ढाई बजे हैं।
८. पौने दस बजे हैं।
९. पौने आठ बजे हैं।
१०. दस बजे हैं।

२३·२
१. शाम के सात बजे हैं।
२. रात के ग्यारह बजे हैं।
३. सुबह के आठ बजे हैं।
४. सुबह के नौ बजे हैं।
५. दोपहर के बारह बजे हैं।
६. चार बजने वाले हैं।
७. छः बजकर बीस मिनट हैं।
८. पाँच बजने में बीस मिनट हैं।
९. ठीक तीन बजे हैं।
१०. लगभग दो बजे हैं।

२३·३
१. इस हफ़्ते
२. अगले हफ़्ते
३. पिछले हफ़्ते
४. आज सुबह
५. आज रात
६. अब
७. कल
८. दिन के दौरान
९. अक्सर
१०. कभी नहीं
११. कभी-कभी
१२. हमेशा
१३. जल्दी
१४. देर से
१५. सबसे पहले

२३·४ Answers vary.

२३·५
१. आपका स्कूल का पहला दिन कब था?
२. ये लोग केरला में कब थे?
३. इस साल दिवाली कब है?
४. आपकी छुट्टी कब है?
५. आदर्श घर कब आती है?

२३·६
१. स्कूल का पहला दिन
२. दूसरी पत्नी/बीवी
३. तीसरी आँख
४. चौथी जगह
५. सातवाँ स्वर्ग
६. सौलवीं मोमबत्ती
७. साठवाँ जन्मदिन
८. सौवीं बार

24 The continuous tense

२४·१
१. Albert Einstein
२. Barack Obama
३. Lucille Ball
४. Meryl Streep
५. E. T.

२४·२
१. summer, गर्मी, ग्रीष्म
२. winter, सर्दी, जाड़ा
३. autumn, शरद, पतझड़
४. spring, बसन्त, बहार
५. monsoon, मानसून
६. for the snowfall to happen, हिमपात होना
७. to rain, बरसात आना
८. to be windy, हवा चलना
९. to be foggy, धुंध होना
१०. to be sunny, धूप होना
११. to be shady, छांव होना
१२. for an earthquake to come, भूकंप आना

२४·३ Some answers may vary.
१. महाद्वीप २. उपमहाद्वीप ३. बसंत ४. पहाड़ ५. नदी ६. रेगिस्तान ७. झरना
८. बरसात, बारिश ९. बिजली १०. तूफान

२४·४
१. मैं जा रहा हूँ/था।
२. मैं जा रही हूँ/थी।
३. तू जा रहा है/था।
४. तू जा रही है/थी।
५. तुम जा रहे हो/थे।
६. तुम जा रही हो/थीं।
७. आप जा रहे हैं/थे।
८. आप जा रही हैं/थीं।
९. हम जा रहे हैं/थे।
१०. हम जा रही हैं/थीं।
११. यह/वह जा रहा है/था।
१२. यह/वह जा रही है/थी।
१३. ये/वे जा रहे हैं/थे।
१४. ये/वे जा रही हैं/थीं।

२४·५   १. आप कब खा रही हैं?   २. कौन पी रहा है?
       ३. सर्दी हो रही है।   ४. गर्मी हो रही है।
       ५. इस साल, मानसून देर से आ रहा है।   ६. बरसात हो रही थी।
       ७. बादल बन रहे थे।   ८. हवा चल रही है।
       ९. भूकंप आ रहा है।   १०. कल धुंध थी।

२४·६   १. मैं आप से एक प्रश्न पूछ रही हूँ।   २. वह पहाड़ पर चढ़ रहा है।
       ३. वह बस से उतर रही थी।   ४. हमें अच्छा महसूस हो रहा है।
       ५. गायक गा रहा था।   ६. वे इस के बारे में सोच रहे हैं।

25   Future tense

२५.१   १. चप्पल   २. नथ   ३. पेटी   ४. चश्मा   ५. गाउन   ६. दुपट्टा   ७. घघरा
       ८. जेब   ९. बुंदे   १०. लॉकेट

२५.२   १. ठीक   २. ठीक   ३. ठीक   ४. ग़लत   ५. ग़लत   ६. ग़लत   ७. ठीक
       ८. ठीक   ९. ग़लत   १०. ठीक

२५.३

	जाना	चलना
मैं (*m.*)	जाऊँगा	चलूँगा
मैं (*f.*)	जाऊँगी	चलूँगी
तू/यह/वह (*m.*)	जाएगा	चलेगा
तू/यह/वह (*f.*)	जाएगी	चलेगी
तुम (*m.*)	जाओगे	चलोगे
तुम (*f.*)	जाओगी	चलोगी
आप/हम/ये/वे (*m.*)	जाएँगे	चलेंगे
आप/हम/ये/वे (*f.*)	जाएँगी	चलेंगी

२५.४   १. नीलम पहाड़ पर चढ़ेगी।   २. क्या आप सोमवार को काम करेंगे?
       ३. हम यह नहीं पहनेंगे।   ४. वे नया घर खरीदेंगे।
       ५. वह स्वैटर बुनेगी।

२५.५   १. मैं बगीचे में हूँगी।   २. हम मटर पनीर लेंगे।
       ३. तुम उसे उसके जन्मदिन पर क्या दोगे?   ४. उस समय वे कहाँ होंगे?
       ५. पैसा/पैसे कौन देगा?   ६. बड़ा दिन कब होगा?

२५.६   १. मैं ज़्यादा नहीं खर्चूँगी।   २. वह/यह चिंता कर रही है।   ३. वह/यह बचा रहा है।
       ४. वे कपड़े दान करेंगे।   ५. हमें क्या मिलेगा?

Reading practice

Translation:

वह अच्छा <u>कर्म</u> है।	That is good <u>karma</u>.
वे कल <u>योग</u> करेंगे।	They will do <u>yoga</u> tomorrow.
<u>पंडित जी/गुरु जी</u> से मिलिए।	Meet the <u>pundit/guru</u>.
मुझे <u>कश्मीरी</u> स्वैटर पसंद हैं।	I like <u>cashmere</u> sweaters.
उसे <u>खाकी</u> रंग पसंद हैं।	He likes the color <u>khakhi</u>.
आज हम <u>बंगले</u> में जाएँगे।	We will go to the <u>bungalow</u> today.
वह दुकान <u>लूट</u> रहा था।	He was <u>looting</u> the shop.
<u>निर्वाण</u> का मतलब क्या है?	What is the meaning of <u>nirvana</u>?

Hindi alphabet
हिन्दी वर्णमाला

Vowels

SHORT		LONG		SHORT		LONG		SHORT		LONG	
अ	a	आ	ā	इ	i	ई	ī	उ	u	ऊ	ū
ऋ	ṛ	ए	e	ऐ	ai	ओ	o	औ	au		
		अं	ṃ					अः	ḥ		

Consonants

	UNASPIRATED		ASPIRATED		UNASPIRATED		ASPIRATED		NASAL		
1	क	k	ख	kh	ग	g	घ	gh			Velar
2	च	c	छ	ch	ज	j	झ	jh			Palatal
3	ट	ṭ	ठ	ṭh	ड	ḍ	ढ	ḍh	ण	ṇ	Retroflex
4	त	t	थ	th	द	d	ध	dh	न	n	Dental
5	प	p	फ	ph	ब	b	भ	bh	म	m	Labial
6	य	y	र	r	ल	l	व	v			Semi-vowels
7	श	ś	ष	ṣ	स	s					Sibilant
8	ह	h									Aspirate/ Glottal
A	ड़	ṛ	ढ़	ṛh							Dotted version: rolling "r"
B	क़	ḳ	ख़	ḳh	ग़	ġ	ज़	z	फ़	f	Dotted version: adapted from Perso-Arabic
C	क्ष	kṣ	त्र	Tr	ज्ञ	jñ	श्र	śra			Combination letters: adapted from Sanskrit